A PRIMER OF HYPNOSIS

A PRIMER OF HYPNOSIS

WITH SPECIAL REFERENCE TO DENTISTRY

S. ROY SMITH L.D.S.

Distributed by:
The British Society of Medical and Dental Hypnosis
c/o 42 Links Road
Ashtead, Surrey, KT21 2HJ

ISBN 0 9505485 0 2

Printed in Great Britain by John Wright & Sons Ltd., at the Stonebridge Press, Bristol

Contents

Dear Dr. Elliott
I went to the Dentist. Like you said and he got the Drill
and drilled my big tooth and then he put this white stuff
on it. I swished the tv on and watched some singing
and dancing soon it was over the next song came on
I watched it for a while and very soon that was
allso over the next peformenice was quite
Different it was magic tricks there were
many funny tricks the first trick was fist
the man showed us a black hat he showed us
inside it and all over but nothing was in
it or on it he put it on his head and
counted two ten then he showed us inside
was a rabbit what a funny trick after that it
was all over the show was finishdand even
the Dentist had finishished I got Down from
the chair the Drill Did not hert it was a very
good program, I only havto go back onece moore
and I will Do the same next time I had
Just been to sundayscool it was fun I hope neyt
time I can watch tv agen and I will.

From Suzanne McNamara

poppa went back to england too day
mummy went too see poppa on the train
it is monday to-day we had a bad storm

Letter received from one of his patients by Dr. Charles Elliott, Brisbane

Preface

For some years the writer has had the intention of writing a short book on hypnosis in dental practice.

Frost's excellent *Hypnosis in General Dental Practice* is no longer available and from the other side of the Atlantic almost if not all the textbooks as applied specifically to dentistry are out of print.

This short volume is in no way to be regarded as definitive but it is sincerely hoped that it will constitute a practical guide to the novitiate and a useful reference in the course of practice.

Considerable attention has been paid to methods of induction and many are, of course, equally suited to the needs of the medical practitioner; indeed an appreciable amount of the subject matter is relevant to both the disciplines.

In order to keep the cost of production down to a reasonable figure it was decided to dispense with illustrations, an omission which the writer feels is of little consequence as illustrations of the textual matter are of small value in hypnotic teaching.

Much material has been taken from textbooks read over the past twenty years—due acknowledgement has been made where possible to the pioneers who blazed the trail.

The opinions and convictions expressed are the writer's own; they may differ sometimes from the accepted but no apology is offered because this variation from what was previously regarded as a standard has been brought about by the writer for one purpose and one only, namely, to leave the subject completely independent of the operator-hypnotist.

Throughout this short book the importance of auto-hypnosis and the safeguarding of the subject's interests have been stressed.

If, as a result of this teaching, each patient is rendered capable of happily experiencing dental treatment *at the hands of his or her chosen dentist*, the writer will have written this book to some purpose.

CHAPTER 1

A Short History of Hypnosis

It is certain that hypnosis in some form or other has been used by man since very early times but as there was no form of rationalised medicine as we now know it, its use was confined entirely to the witch doctor and the like. But the power of suggestion has always been with us and in a remarkable book of exploration *The Rivers ran East*[1] Leonard Clark describes how the witch doctor protects the warrior trekking through the jungle from the bite of a deadly snake.

The warrior wears a charm in the form of a bracelet made from the skin of an iguana: there are two reasons why this is effective, the skin emits a faint odour which, unknown to the wearer, keeps him constantly conscious of the presence of a snake and he subconsciously watches for it. If a snake's head rises close by to strike, the man freezes—stops all motion for he is not afraid, he thinks the charm will protect him. The snake lowers his head and begins to crawl away and he kills it with his knife. The other reason is that a frightened man emits an odour, an odour of fear and snakes are sensitive to it. When it detects this odour the snake itself is afraid and it strikes. Our civilisation cannot dismiss all this so-called mumbo jumbo and there may indeed often be a sound reason behind it.

In a book of this nature space does not permit of a discussion of the various cults, rites etc. of primitive peoples though there may well be in many of their practices a close relationship with hypnosis.

For the purpose of this short history we may regard Anton Mesmer[2] (1734–1815) as the founder of hypnosis as we know it. Mesmer was an Austrian physician who was born in the little village of Iznang on the borders of Lake Constance. We are all familiar with the verb 'to mesmerise' but how many of us know anything about the man himself? The picture most readily called to mind is of a somewhat sinister figure clad in brightly coloured long flowing robes who appeared before his patients in a semi-darkened room with soft music playing. This image is, indeed, in part true but before criticising the man it is important to remember the age in which he lived. The latter part of the eighteenth century was a period in which ignorance, superstition and gullibility still ran rife and the ethical standards of medicine as we now come to think of them were virtually non-existent.

Mesmer was in fact a cultured and erudite man who had spent many years in three universities studying science and philosophy before finally graduating in medicine in Vienna in 1766.

He had many friends among the intelligentsia of his day and formed a lasting friendship with the Mozart family, at whose musical soirées he would perform with considerable effect on the glass harmonica which was essentially an instrument of glass jars or bowls containing water at different levels and the melody was produced by tapping the various containers. Mesmer thought that a magnetic fluid was present in the body and that all disease was due to a disturbance in this fluid. He went to Paris and for a time became quite famous for the clinics that he established there and he undoubtedly had many spectacular cures among some emotionally disturbed people who were suffering from what is now called a psychosomatic disease. Mesmer not unnaturally incurred the wrath and jealousy of the physicians of his day and a commission of enquiry was set up on the orders of Louis the sixteenth; it is interesting to note that the names of Lavoisier, Benjamin Franklin and Dr. Guillotin appear on the commission. Mesmer was discredited as a result of this enquiry and he left France for Switzerland where he died in 1815.

A period now followed when hypnosis was little heard of, but in the first half of the nineteenth century there was a considerable re-awakening of interest and in England John Elliotson (1791–1868) began to practise mesmerism: Elliotson who introduced the stethoscope into this country was Professor of Medicine at University College Hospital. He met with strong opposition, prejudice and even ridicule and eventually he was forbidden to use mesmerism in the hospital. He resigned his appointment in 1838, never again to enter the hospital for which he had done so much. He was a sincere man with strong if sometimes fallacious convictions and his belief in clairvoyance and phrenology gave his opponents plenty of ammunition which they were only too eager to use. Elliotson said that mesmerism was of great use in functional illness and that hysteria was by no means confined to women. For many years he and his supporters produced a paper called the *Zoist* which recorded *inter alia* accounts of operations by Esdaile in India. He died a disappointed man in London in 1868.

JAMES BRAID[3] (1795–1860) was a Scot who had settled in medical practice in Manchester; after witnessing a public demonstration of hypnosis he began experimenting for himself. His name is of considerable importance in the history of hypnosis; he suggested the name 'hypnotism' from the Greek word meaning sleep as being more suitable than mesmerism and he removed much of the ignorance and superstition surrounding the subject.

He used a method of induction known as 'Eye fixation' which is still in use today but his most important contribution lay undoubtedly in the fact that he showed the hypnotic trance to be purely *subjective* in character, that it was due to suggestion alone and in no way with the "magnetic fluids" of Anton Mesmer.

About this time JAMES ESDAILE[4] (1808–1859), a Scottish surgeon in the employ of the East India Company, began to use hypnosis to produce anaesthesia for the many operations he performed on the natives; his success was remarkable and he records some three hundred major operations and over a thousand minor ones using no other anaesthetic. The major operations were mostly for the removal of scrotal tumours. The mortality rate for these operations had been about 50 per cent; Esdaile records 160 cases with a mortality rate of 5 per cent and in no case was death the result of surgery, usually being due later to, in the words of Esdaile "Fever, cholera or like causes".

Apart from surgery he had obtained very successful results in the treatment of functional paralysis. The Indian medical journals refused to publish any of his articles and he left India in 1851 to settle in Perth. At the suggestion of Professor J. Y. Simpson of Edinburgh he sent an account of the 160 cases of scrotal tumour to an English medical journal. This was not published so he then sent a more general paper containing a résumé of his surgical work; this was refused on the grounds that it was unpractical! Esdaile died in Sydenham, London, in 1859 a disillusioned man. His book originally called 'Mesmerism in India' will remain an all-time classic. Meanwhile in France considerable interest had been aroused. A country doctor by the name of A. A. Liébault (1823–1904), who had been inspired by the earlier work of one Baron du Potet and the Englishman Braid, was treating large numbers of his patients in Nancy using hypnosis by direct suggestion. It is said that he cured a patient of sciatica by suggestion and that this so enraged the eminent Professor Bernheim[5] of the School of Medicine in Nancy, as he himself had been unable to effect a cure, that he went to see Liébault to expose "This quack and charlatan". What he saw when he went to this obscure country doctor's clinic so convinced him that he became a staunch supporter and friend.

A school of thought was set up known as the Nancy School. Their views differed considerably from those of the Salpêtrière School under Jean-Martin Charcot (1825–1893). Charcot was a well-known anatomist and neurologist. His patients were mainly hysterics and he claimed quite erroneously as we now know that only these patients were susceptible to suggestion. He had, due to his prestige, a large following which for a time included Sigmund Freud but many of his views were based on false premises and the Nancy School came to be accepted.

Sigmund Freud[6] (1856–1939) was probably one of the greatest minds in any generation and after his visits to Charcot he began to use hypnosis in his psycho-analytical therapy: he experienced some failures due to various causes, became discouraged and abandoned its use in his therapy. As Freud had become a well-known figure by this time hypnosis suffered a severe setback as an adjunct to psycho-therapy.

A whole chapter might well be devoted to Freud but in a work of this kind it will suffice to say that he showed beyond all doubt that the unconscious mind held prisoner a host of memories that had slipped in from the conscious mind and that although they were forgotten they could have an enormous effect on the behaviour of the individual: he further showed that these repressed memories could be recalled in psychoanalysis and that the effect of this purging or catharsis would frequently result in a cure of the condition. Shakespeare in *Macbeth*, Act 4, Scene 3, has Ross say:

> 'What! man; ne'er pull your hat upon your brows;
> Give sorrow words: the grief that does not speak
> Whispers the o'er-fraught heart, and bids it break.'

In a later chapter more will be said about the role of the subconscious but it will be enough at this juncture to say that by means of hypnosis suggestions may be implanted directly into the subconscious mind where they will have the maximum effect in overcoming the patient's fears, phobias etc.

To return once more to the English scene the name of JAMES MILNE BRAMWELL[7] (1852–1925) holds pride of place. He was a Scot who had settled in the Midlands and he was first attracted to the subject by the work of Esdaile and Braid, particularly the former. It is of interest to the dental profession to note that although there are records of tooth extraction before Bramwell's time, he quotes many cases and some are for multiple extractions. There was a report in the March issue of the *British Dental Journal* for 1890 in which one Arthur Turner of Leeds extracted in all forty teeth for various patients who went into hypnosis at Bramwell's suggestion. In one particular case Bramwell was not present and the girl presented herself with a letter from him, Bramwell, which ran:

"Dear Mr. Turner—I send you a patient with enclosed order. When you give it to her, she will fall asleep at once and obey your commands. J. Milne Bramwell.

'Go to sleep by order of Dr. Bramwell, and obey Mr. Turner's commands.'"

Bramwell was a painstaking observer and his book *Hypnotism, Its History, Practice and Theory* contains hundreds of the most carefully recorded case histories and may be read to great advantage today.

In the First World War hypnosis was again used by Brown and Hadfield in the treatment of shell-shock and in the Second World War to a much greater extent by the Americans and one may justly claim that its use in this field is now undisputed.

To explain the decline in the use of hypnosis as a means of producing anaesthesia it is necessary to refer very briefly to the history of this subject.

The story of anaesthesia is both dramatic and tragic—for suffering mankind it brought total relief from pain in operative procedures, and before the mid-nineteenth century any operation was a truly terrifying experience, but for the men who discovered it, it brought nothing but shame, persecution and poverty and to two of them the ultimate tragedy of the unsound mind.

The dental profession may recall with pride that the incalculable benefits of anaesthesia were given to the world by two American dentists.

From the whole unhappy story two names stand out—they are HORACE WELLS (died 1848) and WILLIAM GREEN MORTON (1819–1868). Wells had one of his own teeth extracted under nitrous oxide anaesthesia in 1844, but a demonstration he gave before the Boston Dental Society proved a fiasco as his anaesthetic skills were not unnaturally lacking and so pride of place fell to Morton; on Friday, October 16th, at ten o'clock in the morning at the Massachusetts General Hospital ether was successfully administered to one Gilbert Abbott for the removal of a tumour under the lower jaw. On November 7th Alice Mohan, aged 21, had a leg amputated above the knee, the operation being a complete success, anaesthesia had arrived. The story of these operations has been most vividly described and is one of the most exciting in the annals of medical history.[8]

The news of this and other triumphs soon spread; here surgery had for the first time a means of overcoming pain that was applicable to all cases and so hypnosis fell into disuse.

In general it may be said that in the period between the World Wars very little use was made of hypnosis in the field of dentistry. In November 1938 however ERIC WOOKEY had an article in the *British Dental Journal* entitled 'The Uses and Limitations of Hypnosis in Dental Treatment'. This was a remarkably balanced and far-seeing paper and may be read with advantage today although in the light of nearly thirty years' post-war experience opinions have changed somewhat.

Soon after the Second World War there was a reawakening of interest in dental hypnosis especially in America, and with the establishment of proper teaching courses run under the auspices of the British Society of Medical and Dental Hypnosis throughout the country one may confidently look forward to an ever-increasing use of hypnosis as an adjunct in normal treatment.

REFERENCES

1. CLARK, Leonard. *The Rivers ran East.* Hutchinson, London, 1954.
2. WALMSLEY, D. M. *Anton Mesmer (a biography).* Robert Hale, London, 1967.
3. BRAID, James. *Braid on Hypnotism.* Julian Press, New York, 1960.
4. ESDAILE, James. *Hypnosis in Medicine & Surgery.* Julian Press, New York, 1957.
5. BERNHEIM, HIPPOLYTE, *Suggestive Therapeutics.* Associated Booksellers, Westport, Connecticut, 1957.
6. FREUD, Sigmund. *The Life and Works of Sigmund Freud,* abridged by Ernest Jones. Readers Union, The Hogarth Press, London, 1961.
7. BRAMWELL, James Milne. *Hypnotism, Its History, Practice and Theory.* Julian Press, New York, 1956.
8. MACQUITTY, Betty. *The Battle for Oblivion.* Harrap, London, 1969.

CHAPTER 2

The Uses, Abuses and Limitations of Hypnosis in Dentistry

THE main uses may be roughly classified into the following headings:

1. Securing a degree of total *relaxation* thereby raising the threshold of pain so that treatment that was previously impossible becomes easily tolerable.
2. Production of analgesia in obtaining submission to local anaesthesia.
3. In orthodontia—conditioning children to wear appliances.
4. Gagging with the insertion of the saliva ejector, X-ray film, the taking of impressions etc.
5. The psychological approach to anaesthesia.
6. Minor psychotherapeutic techniques.
7. The control of fainting, haemorrhage and salivation.
8. The ego-strengthening technique.

1. *Relaxation with a Concomitant Raising of the Threshold of Pain*

Unquestionably the relaxation and the raised pain threshold that invariably accompanies it places hypnosis in dental practice in a very favourable light.

Every dentist is familiar with the patient who sits in the chair exhibiting all the signs of fear; his fight or flight mechanism which, phylogenetically, was of survival value in meeting the emergency situation no longer is of use to him in the dental chair. To quote Joseph Landa:[1] 'Nature is not keeping pace in adapting the human being to the numerous complex changes and modifications that human intelligence creates in our environment. Our bodily resources to meet *emergency situations in life* remain almost the same as they were in our ancestry.'

As dentists we all know the nervous patient who spends a large part of his appointment period fidgeting in the chair, swallowing, opening and closing his mouth and forever asking for more mouthwash; the persistent delaying tactics made manifest by a plethora of futile questions being also a dominant feature of these cases. One has only to raise the lip and attempt to wipe the sulcus with a pledget of wool to produce an instant reaction.

Now it may be stressed at the outset that it is by no means always necessary to secure depth in the hypnotic trance for a successful outcome. The acceptance of treatment in a previously nervous patient when in only a light trance is most rewarding and it should not be forgotten that the percentage of patients capable of reaching this stage is very high, probably 90 per cent. Fear of pain has been diminished to a remarkable degree and because in the fear–tension–pain syndrome fear has been all but eliminated the threshold of pain has been significantly raised. Only those who have had the joyful experience of working on a previously nervous patient can appreciate the change that has taken place. It may be stated categorically that it is this application of hypnosis to general dental practice that constitutes the greatest benefit and later in this book the complete approach at conscious and subconscious levels will be fully described.

2. *Production of Analgesia*

Although the pain threshold is raised appreciably by means of relaxation one frequently comes across patients, children in particular, who are unwilling to have injections; the very thought of a needle produces a reaction of fear. In the rare cases of a deep-seated needle phobia it may be necessary to seek psychiatric advice but usually the production of hypnotic analgesia will be all that is needed to secure the patient's cooperation.

This is how it works—the patient is put into a trance which is deepened in the usual way. Analgesia of the hand is produced by one or other of several methods which will be described in another chapter: after testing this analgesia in the hypnotic trance the subject is awakened *but the analgesia is retained as a post-hypnotic phenomenon* and demonstrated to him in the waking state. The psychological effect is naturally very marked. The patient is wide awake, alert, normal in every respect with the exception that one of his hands is numb. He can no longer harbour any doubts that he may have had about hypnosis, for him it works! It is then explained to him that this numbness can be transferred by him to any chosen area in his mouth with the suggestion—'And then, of course, you wouldn't mind having something put into your gum at all would you?' At this stage most subjects will agree and analgesia in the desired area is produced and the injection given. This is a very successful method of securing the patient's co-operation, no doubt because the motivation towards success is very high in dental cases.

3. *In orthodontia—Conditioning Children to Wear Appliances*

A reasonable suggestion that does not run counter to the subject's ethical and moral code that is implanted into the *subconscious mind* will in most cases override a *conscious* desire to the contrary. This fact is of great importance in conditioning: the difficulty in obtaining the child's full co-operation in wearing appliances is commonplace. Children usually rationalise their inability to wear it by saying it is too uncomfortable, they cannot talk properly with it in or that they are ridiculed by their friends etc. Now most dentists are very capable of explaining to young patients the advantages of wearing an appliance; how, for instance, in the case of a girl it will help her to retain her good looks and so forth.

This explanation will carry twice as much weight if it is given in the hypnotic trance and it need only be a light trance—it is seldom necessary to secure depth; a quiet but confident voice with no hint of compulsion pointing out the benefit that will ultimately be obtained will meet the requirements. Repetition at least once will serve, *as in all hypnotic procedure*, to reinforce the suggestion.

This simple method carries a very high degree of success. In this type of hypnotic approach the dental surgeon may regard himself as the teacher and guide, quietly but firmly and confidently leading the subject along a path that leads to success: it leads to success because, although the subject may at times be consciously antagonistic, he is almost always *subconsciously* motivated favourably.

4. *Gagging*

This distressing complaint may occur with the insertion of

the saliva ejector, the water spray, cotton wool rolls, X-ray films (particularly in the area of the upper or lower eights) and the taking of impressions; it is encountered in adults and children. The psychological rejection of treatment is manifest physiologically and the offending article is summarily 'thrown out' as it were. A considerable time may be spent in trying to persuade the patient to accept treatment and very often success is lacking. In hypnosis the dentist has a very powerful ally and here again a deep trance is seldom required which means that success may often be achieved at the first visit.

The same approach may be used for all cases of gagging. The patient is put into hypnosis and suggestions are made to the effect that when he wakes up he will find the saliva ejector (X-ray film, wool roll etc.) does not worry him in the least; he will be able to keep it there as long as is necessary and he will be very pleased about it. As with all forms of suggestive therapeutics this is repeated two or three times with complete conviction and there must be no hint of failure in the manner of the operator's speaking. It may be noted that the subject has been told that he will be very pleased about it; it is of some importance for the subject to realise that in overcoming his difficulties he has gained personal satisfaction. His morale has been boosted; he has been given a metaphorical pat on the back.

5. *The Psychological Approach to Anaesthesia*

It is fully realised that modern anaesthesia with its adjuvants, relaxants and pre-anaesthetic sedatives presents a very different picture from the one to which dental surgeons had reluctantly become accustomed in the years before the Second World War. Nevertheless, as a form of premedication for general anaesthesia, especially in children, hypnosis holds a very high place. In many years of general dental practice the writer has used a form of hypnotic approach using nitrous oxide and oxygen with marked success. Let us take the case of a young child who is about to have an anaesthetic for extractions. The child is seated comfortably in the chair and it is explained to him that he can, if he so wishes, just close his eyes and dream about last year's summer holiday, his Christmas party or indeed anything that he wishes and that when he wakes up his bad tooth will be out. He closes his eyes and is talked to slowly and monotonously and told that he is beginning to see himself on the beach or wherever he has chosen and after a minute or so of patter the nose-piece with the hand cupping it below the rim is held just in front of the nose and the anaesthetic allowed to flow under slight pressure; after another 15 seconds or so of patter the nose-piece is lowered right over the nose and anaesthesia proceeds in the usual way.

It is probable that most anaesthetists develop an approach that is tantamount to the hypnotic approach but in choosing a definite 'image' as it were for the child to grasp we have gone a step further, and it is quite certain that the majority of these children have entered a light trance before they have been anaesthetised and may well remain in hypnosis after the termination of anaesthesia. The degree of psychological trauma is thus reduced to an absolute minimum.

There is currently a revival of interest in *Relative Analgesia*[2] for prolonged conservative dental treatment and it is of interest to mention that Langa in his book of that name has used relative analgesia to bring about the hypnotic trance in subjects who had previously been resistant: the usual post-hypnotic suggestions for future induction were given during analgesia and all the subjects went into hypnosis on subsequent visits.

We may therefore well postulate that this effect is reversible and that the few difficult subjects who do not take readily to relative analgesia may be put into hypnosis, given all the necessary instructions for analgesia and the administration may proceed forthwith or on a subsequent visit. There is scope for considerable clinical experimentation in this field for it must be said that the subject's state of mind in relative analgesia and in hypnosis is running on parallel lines.

6. *Minor Psychotherapeutic Techniques*

Much has been written in the psychiatric literature concerning the evils of *Direct Symptom Removal under Hypnosis* and the dental surgeon has been, quite rightly, repeatedly warned not to see himself as a would-be psychiatrist. It has been said that as direct symptom removal does not deal with the root cause it can be dangerous and the results are seldom if ever permanent. Clinical experience *in suiatble cases* has not justified either of these statements and in dentistry a large measure of success may be attained in curing the subject of certain habits *which no longer serve any useful purpose*. The subject is ready and willing to abandon his habit: in this category one encounters such undesirable habits as *Unilateral mastication*, *Thumb sucking* and *Nail-biting* etc.

The unilateral mastication manifest in the young patient who has had acute ondontalgia in a molar tooth, which for one reason or another went untreated for some weeks with the result that even months afterwards there was a total avoidance of the area, may be speedily and safely cured under hypnosis by pointing out that the cause no longer exists; he is further given positive suggestions that he will remember to eat on both sides of his mouth the very moment he picks up his knife and fork.

Thumb sucking in an otherwise normal child, who has persisted in this habit long after it has ceased to serve any useful purpose, may be dealt with at the hypnotic level with little danger that any adverse substitution will take place; it will not be amiss at this point to clarify what is meant by 'an otherwise normal child'. Irving Secter in *The Practical Application of Medical and Dental Hypnosis* says: 'The child who is at variance with his surroundings, who laughs when he ought to be crying and cries when he ought to be laughing', he is the one to leave well alone or, if you will, send him to the psychiatrist. Now the general practitioner who usually has a considerable background knowledge of the parents and has seen the child grow up will be reasonably able to form an opinion as to his normality. A suitable wording for this form of hypnotherapy will be dealt with in the case histories at the end of the book. Dental surgeons will not, if they are wise, be exploring the subconscious mind seeking latent material which the subject may not be ready or willing to give up: as has been stated elsewhere resentment is unlikely to be caused in dental treatment because the subject in nearly all cases wants to succeed—he is motivated towards success. Hartland in his book *Medical and Dental Hypnosis*[4] points out that in the rare cases where psychiatrical treatment may be necessary it is very unlikely that direct symptom removal would have any effect whatsoever since the subject would be most unlikely to surrender his symptoms which have a strong defence mechanism.

7. *The Control of Fainting, Haemorrhage and Salivation*

Fainting. Hypnosis has proved to be a very useful aid here. Suggestions given in only a light trance have a very marked effect and by suitable wording success may often be attained: Simple suggestions to the effect that—"Now you have learned to relax so well you will realise that you have got rid of all your tension and fear and this was the cause of your faintness and so you will no longer have the least tendency to faint. You will be very pleased indeed to know that having conquered your fear you have overcome your other trouble." Repetition will help to strengthen the effect here as in all suggestive therapy and it may also be noted that the patient has been reminded that in overcoming his fears he experiences pleasure in the achievement.

Haemorrhage. Few controlled experiments have been conducted to prove that bleeding may be favourably influenced by hypnotic suggestion. Schneck in *Hypnosis in Modern Medicine*[5] quotes some experiments in which the clotting time was apparently reduced but the tests were inconclusive: it is probable that the bleeding time can be reduced by direct hypnotic suggestion for it must not be forgotten that the autonomic nervous system may, at the very least, be partially controlled in hypnosis, especially in a deep trance.

In general dental practice most dental surgeons would agree that in those cases where hypnosis was used healing was almost invariably rapid and bleeding presented no problem, but it is, of course, difficult to prove that the same result would not have been achieved without hypnotic suggestions in those particular subjects.

It could well be that the lowered tension, the relaxed condition implicit in the hypnotic situation may in itself be a reason for good healing and lack of haemorrhage. All suggestions for well-being, uneventful recovery etc. ought to be given as routine in operative procedures and therefore the specific inclusion of haemorrhage may well come into this category; it can do no harm and it may be beneficial.

Salivation. Can salivation be controlled under hypnosis? It is the writer's firm opinion that salivation seldom becomes a problem. Every dentist is familiar with the very nervous child who reluctantly opens his mouth when asked to do so and he is equally familiar with the jet of saliva that shoots out of his mouth from the lingual ducts; every roll that is put into his mouth becomes swamped immediately *but* in hypnosis he is a different person, the relaxed condition results in a dramatic lessening of the flow of saliva. The previous remarks concerning haemorrhage apply equally well to salivation.

8. *The Ego-strengthening Technique*

This technique was developed by Hartland and is described in detail in Chapter 15 of his book: he mentions that direct symptom removal is much more likely to be successful if it is preceded by ego-strengthening and, furthermore, any complications will be minimal. He also points out that it may be used to great advantage before the commencement of simple hypnotherapy; such psycho-hypnotherapy as may be used by dental surgeons *when they have gained sufficient experience* and always provided *that their therapy is strictly confined to their own particular discipline.*

John Hartland's complete verbalisation may be considered too lengthy for use in a busy dental practice and he suggests modification in length and if need be words to suit the operator. The writer has used a shortened version for many years as a routine in practice. The actual words are almost entirely Hartland's but many passages have been deleted for the sake of brevity.

The following is a suggested routine:

'You have now become *so* deeply relaxed . . . *so* deeply asleep . . . that your mind has become *so* sensitive . . . *so* receptive to what I say . . . that *everything* that I put into your mind . . . will sink *so* deeply into the unconscious part of your mind . . . and will cause *so* deep and lasting an impression there . . . that *nothing* will eradicate it.'

The writer then proceeds:

'Every day . . . you will become *more* alert . . . *more* wide awake . . . *more* energetic . . . you will become *much* less easily tired . . . *much* less easily fatigued . . . *much* less easily discouraged. *Every day* your nerves will become *stronger and steadier. Every day* you will become *so deeply interested* in what you are doing . . . *so deeply interested* in whatever is going on . . . that your mind will become *much* less preoccupied with yourself . . . and you will become *much* less conscious of yourself . . . and your own feelings.

'*Every day* . . . your mind will become *much calmer and clearer* . . . *more* composed . . . *more* placid . . . *more* tranquil.

'You will become *much* less easily worried . . . *much* less easily agitated . . . *much* less fearful and apprehensive . . . *much* less easily upset.

'You will be able to think *more* clearly . . . you will be able to concentrate *more* easily . . . your memory will improve . . . and you will be able to see things in their true perspective . . . without magnifying them . . . without allowing them to get out of proportion.

'*Every day* you will become emotionally *much* calmer . . . *much* more settled . . . *much* less easily disturbed.

'And *every day* . . . you will feel a *greater* feeling of personal well-being . . . a *greater* feeling of personal safety and security . . . than you have felt for a long time . . . a long long time.

'*Every day* you will become . . . *and you will remain* . . . more and more completely relaxed . . . both *mentally and physically* . . . *even when you are no longer with me.*

'And as you become . . . and *as you remain* . . . more relaxed and less tense each day . . . so you will develop *much more* confidence in yourself . . . *much more* confidence in your ability to do . . . not only that which you have to do each day . . . but also . . . *much more* confidence in your ability to do whatever you ought to be able to do . . . without fear of failure . . . without fear of consequences . . . without unnecessary anxiety . . . without uneasiness.

'Because of this . . . *every day* . . . you will feel *more and more* independent . . . *more* able to 'stick up for yourself' . . . 'to stand upon your own feet' . . . 'to hold your own' . . . no matter how difficult or trying things may be.

'And . . . because all these things will happen . . . exactly as I tell you they will happen . . . you are going to feel *much* happier . . . *much* more contented . . . *much* more cheerful . . . and optimistic . . . *much* less easily discouraged . . . much less easily depressed.'

There are one or two points that may with advantage be noted in connection with this verbalisation: it has been said earlier that repetition is no bad thing in suggestive therapy and you will notice that what Hartland has done is to take a word like tired and say: 'You will become much less easily tired', then go on to say: 'You will become much less easily fatigued' and finally: 'You will become much less weary.' Thus one has two or even three sentences which express more or less the same idea avoiding however the use of the same word; the effect of 'driving home' the idea in a quiet but confident voice with suitable pauses has a very strong influence on the patient's subconscious.

There must be no hurry in giving hypnotic suggestions; in fact it is true to say that one of the cardinal errors in talking to subjects in hypnosis is to hurry. Leave time between each suggestion for the preceding one to sink in.

The dental surgeon who is new to hypnosis may well think that this technique is a waste of time but experience has taught otherwise and indeed once the operator has made himself completely familiar with the verbalisation very little time is needed.

Lastly in this connection the use of the cassette tape recorder will prove an invaluable aid in perfecting delivery.

The Abuses and Dangers of Hypnosis in Dentistry

These are put under one heading because, in the main, the dangers are brought about by the operator himself and ought never to occur: abuse may, of course, be occasioned by the subject or even a third party but it is easy to guard against this eventuality.

To return to the operator, it is the writer's firm opinion that dental surgeons should not use hypnosis in practice unless they have taken a proper course of instruction such as is regularly given by the *British Society of Medical and Dental Hypnosis*. It is *not* sufficient merely to have glanced through induction techniques in a textbook; any operator who uses hypnosis in his practice must remember that he is dealing with the subconscious mind and that he must be fully aware of the significance of any suggestion planted therein. It is a *sine qua non* to the use of hypnosis in dentistry that the dentist confines it strictly within the limits of his own discipline—the exception being the broad spectrum of ego-strengthening—and on no account allows himself to be persuaded by eager patients to attempt various cures either to please them *or to satisfy his own ego.*

Hypnosis should not be used when there is no need for it, the patient who is completely adjusted to accept all forms of dental treatment may be left to his own devices.

The demonstration of hypnotic induction to lay audiences by medical and dental practitioners is considered an abuse of privilege as it is impossible in a single lecture of this type to remove the aura of mysticism that may well be created in the lay mind.

There is virtually no danger in using hypnosis in dentistry and nobody has failed to come out of the trance in the dental chair: the patient has been suitably prepared by the so-called mind set and he knows what to expect. Furthermore, he is motivated towards success, he does not want to fail, he has in fact everything to gain by succeeding (and this may not always be so in hypno-psychotherapy) and the chances therefore of precipitating a psychotic episode are negligible.

In those rare cases where the dental surgeon has doubts as to the normality of his patient it would be wiser to avoid hypnosis altogether and if necessary seek psychiatric advice. It may be mentioned here that the taking down of short case histories before hypnosis is used will prove well worth while; this will be dealt with in the next chapter.

Abuse by the subject or by a third party is not a factor of importance if the operator has been properly trained. The total protection of the subject lies in the important fact that '*If the subconscious mind of an individual in hypnosis accepts a suggestion that is compatible with the moral and ethical code of that individual then the conscious mind will be unable to override it*'.

Suggestive therapeutics owes much to EMIL COUÉ (1857–1926),[6] a French pharmacist, who practised auto-suggestion in Nancy. He is best remembered for his famous maxim: 'Every day, in every respect, I am getting better and better.'

One of the laws of suggestion that he put forward was called the *Law of Dominant Effect* which stated that any idea tends to be realised and that a stronger emotion will always take precedence over a weaker one. 'When the imagination and the will are in conflict the imagination will always win.' Substitute *subconscious* for imagination and *conscious* for will and it may be stated that *any conflict between the subconscious and the conscious mind results in a win for the subconscious.*

To protect the subject from all abuse specific suggestions under hypnosis may be given to him to the effect that 'Now as you sit there, calm and relaxed just listening to my voice, I want you to accept some suggestions that are entirely for your own good. The ability to relax that you have now acquired is of great use to you but it must never be abused. What you have learned is for you alone and it would be wrong of you to allow any person other than a doctor, dentist or a psychiatrist to attempt to put you into this pleasant relaxed state and if they did try you would not permit yourself to relax. Similarly you would on no account go into hynposis at a party to please your friends or at any meeting except a medical or dental one. I am going to repeat what I have said and then I want you to signify that you have understood it all and that you will faithfully abide by these conditions because as I have already explained these instructions are entirely for your own good.'

After these instructions have been repeated the patient's acceptance is obtained, preferably by the method known as *Ideomotor Activity or Signalling*. Cheek and LeCron in their book *Clinical Hypnotherapy*[7] attach great importance to this technique and the writer has found it to be of immense value in obtaining information without creating a traumatic episode.

REFERENCES

1. LANDA, Joseph S. *The Dynamics of Psychosomatic Dentistry*. Dental Items of Interest Pub. Co., Henry Kimpton, London, 1953.
2. LANGA, Harry. *Relative Analgesia in Dental Practice*. W. B. Saunders, London, 1968.
3. ERICKSON, Milton, HERSHMAN, Seymour, and SECTER, Irving. *The Practical Application of Medical and Dental Hypnosis*. Julian Press, New York, 1961.
4. HARTLAND, John. *Medical and Dental Hypnosis*, 2nd edition. Baillière, Tindall, London, 1971.
5. SCHNECK, Jerome M. *Hypnosis in Modern Medicine*, 3rd edition. Charles Thomas, Springfield, Illinois, 1963.
6. COUÉ, Emil. *Better and Better Every Day*. Unwin Books, 1960.
7. CHEEK, David and LECRON, Leslie. *Clinical Hypnotherapy*. Grune & Stratton, London & New York, 1968.

CHAPTER 3

The Presentation of Hypnosis to the Patient and the Mind Set

The Technique of Induction

The Presentation of Hypnosis and the Mind Set

Many pages have been devoted in the various treatises explaining in considerable detail how the patient is conditioned, as it were, to accept hypnosis.

Now in dentistry in particular *Motivation* plays a very large part and it is indeed fortunate for us that almost all our patients are motivated towards a successful goal: certain misconceptions and fears do, however, in many cases require to be cleared up but it is the writer's firm opinion that the most important factor in securing co-operative acceptance is the patient's own 'summing-up' or estimation of the operator and his practice, be this at conscious or subconscious level. This acceptance value will obviously be more favourable with patients who have been coming to the practice for some time but are being newly introduced to hypnosis. Apart from one or two minor fears which are easily dealt with these patients are very willing to co-operate in induction.

The importance of what is called the *Mind Set* has been stressed in many textbooks, and some writers consider it to be a vital factor in winning the confidence of a doubtful subject. Obviously it is necessary to set any doubts or fears that the patient may have at rest and here the busy practitioner may save himself valuable time by preparing a cassette recording of a suitable mind set or having copies printed. The former may be played to patients in the dental office, recovery room or second surgery if vacant. The printed copy may be given to the patient to take home so that his opinion and any remaining doubts may be expressed on his next visit.

I may say that experience has shown these doubts to be minimal. The following is a suggested mind set; it is primarily the work of Mr. Eric Wookey supplemented by the present author and I am indebted to Eric Wookey for permission to print.

Mind Set

There is nothing magical or mysterious about hypnosis. It might be described as a condition somewhat akin to sleep, but it is, of course, not sleep. The hypnotised person is never unconscious and he always listens to the voice of the hypnotist.

It is a condition of considerably increased *Suggestibility* and may be likened to the feeling one has when one is half-awake in the morning. The conscious mind is drowsy, as it were, and suggestions are able to reach the subconscious mind with much greater effect.

There are one or two factors that may constitute a drawback to success. One is a too analytical mind and this tends to occur if you have had a scientific training; it is fatal to success if you stop and ask yourself *why* a certain effect is taking place. If it is suggested that your eyes are feeling tired and that you will want to close them—just let them close, don't go into the how and why of it. The other factor is a fear that when you are drowsy you may be made to say things that you would not normally do or say. Now there is no foundation for this in fact and if any suggestions were made to you that were incompatible with your conscious moral code you would reject them or wake up.

Now in a state of complete relaxation, one can, by means of suggestion, remove the control of the conscious mind to a very large extent and one can achieve such astonishing results as, for instance, the blocking of pain sensations from reaching the brain by simply saying: 'You will feel nothing.' This then is the underlying principle in the state of deep relaxation which we are going to try to induce—to get your conscious mind so drowsy and sleepy that suggestions made for your benefit will get through to your subconscious mind to take the maximum effect.

We achieve this by asking you to concentrate your whole attention and thought on one object, by looking at it. This brings about the state of relaxation and drowsiness which can be of considerable benefit to you. It is a very pleasant feeling indeed.

Lastly you need have no fear that any unscrupulous person would be able to put you into hypnosis, as you cannot be forced into this state. You go into hypnosis for yourself because you wish to learn to relax and furthermore safeguarding suggestions will be implanted into your subconscious mind by me, your teacher and guide, which would make any abuse impossible.

In the course of everyday practice and particularly as experience is gained one finds that hypnosis may be used without any prior conditioning in a number of cases.

Mention may be made at this point of a question that is often asked by students at courses and members at BDA meetings—Do you tell your patients you are using hypnosis? Many pages have been written on this matter, much that is inconclusive. If they have been given a copy of the mind set or listened to the cassette recording they know you are using hypnosis and in most cases their doubts have been cleared up. My own view is as follows:

Firstly, in the case of children the parent may be approached and permission asked to teach relaxation: Picture Visualisation (p. 29) is very briefly explained. The parent may well ask at this stage—'Are you going to hypnotise her?' Here a short explanation to the effect that some people would say it was hypnosis and others that it was a state of deep relaxation may be given. One may add that in this deep state of relaxation the child is fantasizing the TV picture she has chosen so much so that dental treatment becomes of secondary importance. The parent may be further told that he or she is welcome to come into the surgery later when the patient has been taught to relax and see how pleasant and enjoyable it is. It is seldom once a reasonable explanation has been given that parental opposition is encountered. Adults may be told that hypnosis is really a form of extreme relaxation, that they may go into it as a result of the suggestions they receive or they may be simply very deeply relaxed. Despite all that has been said in the textbooks concerning the preparation of the patient the writer in twenty years of practice has found very little opposition from would-be subjects in accepting hypnosis and often 'At first sight'.

Before explaining the various methods of hypnotic induction it is necessary to say a few words concerning the time involved in preliminary procedures and the subsequent training. Firstly, there is obviously the financial consideration because if 3–4 patients are seen every week for whom no charge is made the loss is appreciable.

Secondly, in a very busy practice it may sometimes be very difficult to fit these extra appointments in and at the same time maintain an 'even flow' in the treatment of the remaining patients. This latter problem is one that each practitioner will have to decide for himself and will depend on his own individual type of practice.

To go back to the financial aspect—it must not be forgotten that once the patient is trained to accept treatment under hypnosis a very appreciable amount of time may, nay will, be saved; it is only those dentists who have treated a previously nervous and tense patient who can experience the full satisfaction in treating that same patient when he has been trained to relax fully.

The NHS does not, except in rare cases which, from a practical point of view, need not concern us here, allow any extra fee for dental treatment under hypnosis.

If the patient has expressed a wish to learn to relax and it is the considered opinion of the operator that it would be of benefit to the patient, the writer then has explained the position *vis-à-vis* the NHS and agreed upon a fee for each visit *prior to acutal treatment under the Service*.

In the case of children the writer has treated very many of them without fee because they usually consume very little time initially and subsequent treatment proves to be a reward in itself.

Looking back over forty years of general dental practice the writer would have undoubtedly saved many hours had he practised hypnosis as an adjunct to conservative treatment during the first twenty years. But the whole question of fees earned in hypnosis is a very complex one and taking all the varied considerations that apply to individual practices the ultimate decision rests with the practitioner himself. In cases where a patient is referred to a particular practitioner for hypnotic conditioning, later to be sent back to the original dental surgeon, a fee must, of course, always be charged and it should be made clear that each visit will be charged.

Before actual dental treatment may be commenced 2–3 visits may be required for hypnotic conditioning, but these need not be of very long duration; as a practical guide 15 or 20 minutes at the most may be given up to each session.

One must never forget that once conditioned a patient will submit willingly year after year to all dental treatment and this factor alone goes a long way to justify the initial time spent.

Induction Techniques

The following induction techniques are well tried and have proved very successful in practice: the list is by no means exhaustive but should enable the practitioner to meet most eventualities. One method may fail, another will succeed, and although it is true to say that most operators tend to favour a particular method it is nevertheless very useful in the event of a failure to have at least one or two alternatives. An easy method of learning to apply two or three induction techniques in the early stages of one's hypnotic practice is explained later in this book (p. 40).

A little thought will make it clear that an induction involving a vivid imagination is unlikely to succeed in a subject who possesses poor visual imagery; it would be far wiser to choose the dropped-coin technique.

1. Erickson's arm levitation.
2. A modification of the above.
3. Eye-fixation plus distraction.
4. Picture visualisation.
5. Visual imagery.
6. The coin technique (the dropped coin).
7. Relaxation through the release of tension.
8. Relative analgesia used for the hypnotic induction of completely resistant patients.
9. Eye closure (after Elman).

1. *Erickson's Arm Levitation*

This method, developed by Milton Erickson in 1928, is considered by Lewis Wolberg in the *Medical Hypnosis*, Volume 1,[1] to be the best of all procedures; perhaps the main drawback is that it is somewhat time-consuming and also may require an appreciable effort on the part of the operator in a few cases.

What follows is more or less a transcription from Wolberg:

'I want you to make yourself comfortable in the chair and let yourself relax. Bring both your hands palms down on your thighs—that's right. Now just keep watching your hands, observe them closely. As you do you will notice certain things that happen in the course of relaxing. They have always happened when you relax but you have not noticed them before. I will point them out to you. Now concentrate all your thoughts, all your attention on your hands. Think of the feelings, the sensations in your hands no matter what they are. Perhaps you feel the heaviness of your hand as it lies on your thigh or just the pressure. It may be that you notice the texture of your trousers as they press against your hand and fingers or the warmth of your hand penetrates through the material and you feel it on your thigh. There could be a tingling sensation in your hand which spreads to your fingers. Observe these feelings whatever they are. Keep watching your hand and you notice how still and quiet it is and you begin to wonder when the motion that is there will show itself. It will be interesting to see where the movement will first manifest itself, which of your fingers will move first. It may be the middle finger, the forefinger, the ring finger or the little finger or the thumb. One of the fingers is going to jerk or move. You don't know when or where, possibly it will be in the right hand. Let us concentrate our gaze on the right hand for a moment. There! the thumb jerks and moves, it has spread out away from the forefinger. Now you begin to notice something very interesting indeed; as you watch the fingers of your right hand the spaces between the fingers slowly widen, the spaces get wider and wider, all the time wider and wider. You don't try to make it happen, you don't try to stop it happening and as you look at your hand now you see that the fingers have spread out and they are quite widely separated. Your eyes are beginning to feel tired and you feel you would like to close them, but don't let them close, not until I ask you to. You're doing this exercise very well, very well indeed. You become aware as you keep watching your hands that your fingers have a feeling that they want to arch up from your thigh, the tips of your fingers no longer seem to be pressing on the material of your trousers. Look! your index finger has lifted up a little, there is a lightness coming into all the fingers and they begin to rise up too, slowly but surely they rise up, lighter and lighter, they feel very light and the lightness creeps into your hand, your whole hand is beginning to feel light now and your hand is beginning to rise slowly up into the air, as light as a feather; it feels as though a balloon were tied to your wrist with a piece of string and is lifting it up into the air, higher and higher, lighter and lighter! Keep watching your hand and arm as it rises up and up into the air and as it does so you notice that you begin to get tired and sleepy, you would like to close your eyes and let yourself relax but please keep them open until I ask you to let them close and then when they do you will be able to enjoy the peaceful relaxed feeling to the full. Your eyelids get very heavy, breathe deeply in—and out and now as you watch your hand you notice that your arm is beginning to bend and your hand is slowly coming nearer and nearer to your face, closer and closer, up and up and your whole body is experiencing a lovely feeling of relaxation, a sense of drowsiness is creeping over your body and your eyes begin to blink. All the time your arm bends a little bit more and your hand rises nearer and nearer to your face: you keep looking at your hand but you can hardly keep your eyes open but don't let them close yet, not until your hand touches your face and then your eyes close, your hand drops down onto your lap and you sink right down into the chair deeply and wonderfully relaxed, the most relaxed feeling you have ever known.'

This is a very excellent method for those who really feel confident in its use: a suggested way of gaining familiarity with it is to make a cassette recording and act the part out for oneself.

2. *The Raised-arm Technique*

This is quick, simple and successful in most cases. Unlike the last method, instead of the arm rising up and culminating in the fingers touching the face, the raised arm drops down to touch the face.

The arm is raised above the head, the elbow slightly bent so that the head must be tipped well back in order to focus on the fingers. This method is, of course, ideally suited to the dental chair which may with advantage be tilted back appreciably so that the hand is *directly above* the eyes, a slight strain being placed on the eyes in order to focus on the fingers and also gravity is on the operator's side!

What follows is a suggested pattern for verbalisation:

'Throughout this exercise I want you to keep your eyes fixed on your fingers which are quite straight and close together with the thumb pulled down, fingers quite straight and close together—now you can take your own time in relaxing by closely watching your fingers; when you are ready to start relaxing you'll notice some movement in one or other of your fingers, it may jerk slightly at first and then spread apart from the next finger. I will bring this to your notice and you will see how you begin to relax more and more. All right? good! Now keep your eyes glued to your fingers—fingers close together, thumb apart. Breathe slowly and deeply, in—out, in—out. Soon you will notice a slight movement in one or other of your fingers and a space will appear.' This last sentence may be repeated at intervals once or twice and it may be suggested that the eyes are getting tired looking at the fingers and, if they begin to blink, attention may be drawn to this fact but you do not want them to close at this stage so you may say so. 'There! your index finger has moved slightly all of its own accord and there is a space between it and the next finger. Now all the fingers are separating and your eyes feel very tired, your eyelids very heavy but don't let your eyes close yet, just keep watching your fingers and, as you do, you notice that your arm is very slowly bending so that your hand is coming nearer and nearer to your face; it seems almost as though a magnet was attracting your hand like a piece of steel: as your hand comes nearer to your face you blink more and more and soon your hand will touch your face and that will be the signal for your eyes to close, for your arm to flop down into your lap and you sink down in the chair very, very deeply relaxed indeed. There! your fingers touch your face, your eyes close, you feel beautifully relaxed, warm and comfortable.'

In rare cases where there is a final hesitation on the part of the subject, the wrist may be taken and guided down on to the cheek or forehead saying in a quiet but firm voice—'Just close your eyes, let your eyes close, relax yourself completely.' The arm may be given a slight push so that it falls somewhat heavily upon the lap. This seldom fails to produce the trance state.

3. *Eye-fixation plus Distraction*

This is a modified version of John Hartland's eye-fixation method described in his excellent book *Medical and Dental Hypnosis*.

A similar method without distraction is also described but as this only involves the conscious mind with one task I have omitted it believing that suggestions can slip more readily into the subconscious when the conscious is fully occupied.

Now as some form of eye-fixation is used in many induction techniques a practical arrangement that the writer employs may be of interest. A small circular wooden block about 10 cm in diameter, such as is used to hold ceiling roses for electric lights, is pinned or glued to the ceiling above the dental chair; this is painted black to contrast strongly with the surroundings. The spotlight on your unit, if you have one, may be focused on it. The block should be placed well back so that a slight strain is caused in fixating upon it.

The verbalisation now follows:

'I want you to lie back comfortably in the chair. I want you to look upwards at the small circle above your head, the small black circle above your head. Don't let your eyes wander from it for a moment, not for a single moment, just keep looking at it.

'Now I want you to start counting slowly backwards from 300. Mentally, to yourself . . . not out loud.

'Keep on counting . . . slowly and rhythmically . . . and go on counting until you hear me tell you to stop.

'Try not to listen to me . . . any more than you can help. You'll still hear everything I say . . . but try not to listen. Just stick to your counting.

'Let yourself go completely limp and slack . . . limp and slack. Breathe quietly . . . in . . . and out.

'And whilst you're breathing quietly . . . in . . . and out . . . you can feel that your eyes are becoming very, very tired. They may feel a little watery . . . the black circle may begin to look a little blurred.

'Already your eyelids are beginning to feel very, very heavy and tired.

'Presently they will want to blink.

'As soon as they start to blink . . . just let them blink as much as they like.

'You see! They're starting to blink now.

'Just let everything happen . . . exactly as it wants to happen. Don't try to make it happen . . . don't try to stop it happening. Just let everything please itself.

'Presently your blinks will become slower. And as they do so . . . your eyes will become more and more tired. The eyelids heavier . . . and heavier. So heavy . . . that they feel they are wanting to close.

'As soon as they feel they want to close . . . let them go . . . just let them close . . . entirely on their own.

'They're wanting to close now . . . let them go . . . closing tighter and tighter . . . tighter and tighter.

'*Go to sleep!*

'Sleep very, very deeply.

'Relax completely . . . and give yourself up to this very pleasant . . . relaxed . . . drowsy feeling.

'Stop counting now . . . stop counting now . . . just relax very very deeply. I pick up your arm . . . as I move it about it is limp, limp as that of a rag doll . . . it just flops about . . . as though there were no joints in your arm . . . and when I let it go it drops down with a flop onto your lap and you go down deeper and deeper into a beautifully relaxed state.'

4. *Picture Visualisation*

This method is particularly suited to children who spend a not inconsiderable part of their lives in a world of fantasy: it may, of course, be equally well applied to many adults. Now that almost every home has a television nothing becomes easier than to talk the young patient down into the picture that he or she has chosen: the operator need, of course, have no knowledge of the chosen picture.

One proceeds somewhat after the following manner:

'Many little boys and girls who come to have their teeth done, don't worry about it in the least, they simply sit back comfortably in the chair, close their eyes and have a lovely dream and in their dream they see the television picture that they have chosen. It's great fun! Wouldn't you like to try it? What is your favourite programme? I'm sure you have one.' Having elicited the picture of choice one may proceed—'As you sit there with your eyes closed feeling warm and comfortable, completely relaxed, thinking all the time about your television programme you will soon begin to see the picture; think very hard about it and soon you will begin to see it in your mind and when you feel you have got it I want you to raise your left hand a little from your lap just to show me you are seeing it.' Usually after a very little reinforcement the fingers begin to rise a little from the lap. One continues: 'That's right, that's very good, now you are beginning to see the picture, just put your hand down. I want you to breathe in . . . and out . . . in . . . and out. Slowly and deeply and as you breathe out you will feel yourself going deeper and deeper into sleep but seeing the picture clearer and clearer, all the time clearer and clearer, clearer and brighter.' The expression on the child's face will by now be one of complete relaxation and further deepening of the trance state may be quickly secured by *arm levitation*. 'As you sit there so warm and comfortable just listening to my voice and see the picture very clearly you will notice a funny thing, you will notice that the fingers of your right hand begin to feel very light and as you think about it the lightness creeps into your whole hand so that it feels as light as a feather, it has no weight at all; it is as though a balloon were tried to your wrist and is pulling your hand and arm up into the air. It is rising up now, light as a feather, it floats up and up and you have a far-away feeling; it is very pleasant indeed. And now your elbow has started to bend and your fingers are slowly coming towards your face, soon your hand will touch your face and then your arm will drop down to your lap again and you will be very deeply asleep but seeing the picture very clearly and always listening to my voice. The picture is just as clear as it is at home now.'

The young patient, instead of looking at a TV programme, may elect to visualise a summer holiday or a Christmas party. The principle is exactly the same, although in the case of, say, a summer holiday at the seaside the writer usually jogs the child's memory with a few suggestions to complete the picture—

'It is warm and sunny on the beach but there is a light breeze blowing; it is low tide and as you walk along you notice how the breeze causes little ripples on the shallow pools of water. You see one or two bathers wading out to reach the deeper water and as you look out to sea you notice the "white horses" on the waves. Further out there are a lot of small sailing boats with red sails, the red sails caught in the sun makes it very easy to see them. They are probably in a sailing race . . . you nod your head to tell me that you can see them.'

It will be noticed that a direct question is not put to the child, all that is asked for is confirmation that the boats are seen. An extension of this concept follows.

'I want you to think of a balloon, it is looped to your wrist with a piece of long white string . . . tell me, what is the colour of your balloon?' You have assumed that he has visualised a balloon and the subject in order to tell you the colour must, if he has not already done so, visualise it at once. This method may be used to great advantage in hypnotic procedure.

5. *Visual Imagery*

This visualisation technique is well described in Irwin Shaw's *Clinical Applications of Hypnosis in Dentistry*.[2] It is very successful particularly with subjects whose mental images are usually seen in colour.

The operator tells the subject—'I want you please to close your eyes and to keep them closed throughout the whole of this exercise as it is much easier to concentrate with closed eyes. I want you to think of a blackboard, I want you to visualise a blackboard, the sort of blackboard you knew when you were at school: at the bottom left-hand side there is a small wooden tray with some pieces of chalk in it, they are of different colours and also there is a yellow duster lying across one corner. You nod your head to tell me that you can see this picture . . . good! Now I want you to go over to the board and pick up a piece of chalk out of the tray, any colour you like, and draw something on the blackboard, something quite simple that will not take too long, it doesn't matter what it is. When you have finished the drawing please nod your head to let me know. . . . Very good! Now put the chalk back in the tray, pick up the yellow duster and rub out what you have just drawn, rub it out carefully and then put the duster back on the tray. Look closely at the blackboard again. Tell me what do you see?' A good subject will say that he sees a smudge left by the duster on rubbing out the drawing. If the subject says that he sees nothing, say: 'Please look again, take a much closer look, don't you see the faint smudge left by your duster? Nod your head when you *do* see it.' The co-operative patient who has nodded his head all along in agreement should now nod his head after taking a closer look. 'That's fine! Now turn your back to the blackboard and look straight in front of you. You see a vase full of very attractive flowers standing on a table . . . you nod your head to tell me that you see it clearly. . . . About how many flowers are there in the vase? What colour are they, are they all the same colour? Good! Now just show me with your hands how long the stems are. That's very good, very good indeed, you've done very well! Now let us turn back to the clean blackboard and you will see everything black, grey, green or any colour you wish. Make your mind blank, relax your mind, clear your mind of all thoughts and just see this colour. Let your whole body relax, relax all over and breathe deeply; take a very deep breath and hold it as long as you comfortably can and then let it out very slowly feeling how you relax deeper and deeper as you do so. I am going to count slowly up to five and as I count you feel yourself relaxing more and more, your whole body gets heavy with the weight of relaxation and when I reach five you will be deeply relaxed far away, warm and comfortable.' This last part may be repeated three times.

It is interesting to note that some subjects exhibit motor activity in performing this exercise: they go through the motions of picking up the chalk, drawing some object in front of them, putting the chalk back in the box and then rubbing the drawing out with the duster, finally replacing the duster. Many subjects do not show any motor activity during this exercise (other than demonstrating the length of the stems) but they may prove good subjects; some, of course, will fail. The writer has never experienced an induction failure in a subject who has manifest motor activity.

There are many other techniques employing visual imagery but this is one of the simplest to carry out.

6. *The Coin Technique* (*the Dropped Coin*)

The writer considers this to be one of the most useful ways of demonstrating hypnotic induction: it was first described in *The Practical Application of Medical and Dental Hypnosis* which is a joint work by Erickson, Hershman and Secter. The success of this method probably lies in the fact that if the subject follows out the instructions to the letter he will almost certainly slip into hypnosis as a matter of course.

The verbalisation now follows:

'I am going to place this coin in your hand, then I ask you to close your fingers gently over it and turn your hand over. Hold it only tightly enough so that the coin doesn't fall to the ground. All right? Good! Now we stretch your arm straight out in front of you and you keep it there please. You'll find that very simple to do. Your thumb is extended right away from the hand. Now here is the first instruction. You are to keep your eyes fixed on that thumbnail, right through the exercise until I suggest otherwise. Your eyes are going to be glued to your thumbnail all the time. Right?

'I'm going to start counting now and with each count you will feel changes in the fingers of your hand. While your eyes are occupied with this thumb, your mind can pay attention to the feelings in your fingers, to the relation of the fingers to the coin, how the fingers feel against the coin, and the feeling of relaxation and looseness that follows. Now as I count allow your fingers to relax and straighten out with each count just a little more, a little more with each count, so that eventually the fingers straighten out to a point where the coin drops to the floor. When the coin drops that is the signal for two things to happen; first for your eyes to close; second for your whole body to go limp and melt right down into the chair, just as if you were going to sleep, into a deep, deep sleep.

'Sometimes, though, the eyes get so heavy from being glued to your thumbnail, so tired, that they close long before the coin drops. That's fine, if it happens. If your eyes close before the coin drops, let them stay closed. Then you can pay all your attention to the way your fingers feel and the way they are relaxing round the coin, relaxing more and more with each count. I'm going to repeat these instructions so that you can follow them exactly. You keep your eyes glued on the thumbnail.

I count and as I count you pay attention to your fingers and feel them straightening out and relaxing. They relax more and more with each count until the fingers have opened to a point where the coin drops. Then unless your eyes are already closed they close now and you go deeply relaxed. The thud of the coin on the floor takes you down into an even deeper relaxed state. I will hold my hand under your arm so that you don't have to fear to relax. Now I think you've understood these instructions thoroughly so we'll just go ahead and you can do your part.

'One! . . . pay attention to your fingers and feel the nice relaxation that's going to come into them . . . with each count a little bit more . . . your eyes are glued to your thumbnail and your fingers relax a little bit more with each count. They are relaxing a little now and your eyes are getting tired and heavy looking at your thumbnail . . . soon they will want to close . . . they're starting to blink . . . it's perfectly all right to let them close. Two! . . . eyes getting heavier, fingers straightening out, you're doing very well. Three! . . . eyes are beginning to water a little now, your eyelids are blinking and your fingers have opened a little more round the coin, you're doing very well indeed. You're making an excellent subject. Four! . . . you can hardly keep your eyes open, fingers straightening out more and more. Five! . . . eyelids closing, fingers opening. It's perfectly all right for you to close your eyes any time you want to. Six! . . . fingers straightening right out, your eyes are closing and your eyeballs are rolling up. You're doing fine! Let your eyes close now . . . very good! [the coin drops to the floor and the eyes have closed]. Breathe slowly and deeply. With each breath that you take feel yourself relax more and more [catch arm as it drops]. Now when I let go of your arm you will feel the heaviness of it pulling it down towards your lap; it just flops down onto your lap when I let it go and that takes you down into a really deeply relaxed state. . . . There! [lets arm drop]. Just sit there and enjoy that calm comfortable feeling of complete relaxation.'

This same coin technique may be used on children, even quite young ones, but for the very young the writer prefers a modification which is also described by Shaw[2] in his book. After the child's confidence has been gained and he has expressed his willingness to take part in the "sleep game" the operator draws something on the back of the right thumbnail, what he draws is not very consequential (the writer draws, very badly, the head of a cat with a felt pen!). The arm is stretched out in front of the child slightly above the horizontal and he is told to look at the drawing all the time without blinking. The operator continues: 'I am going to count up to a hundred and you keep looking at the drawing on your thumbnail. Soon your eyes will get heavy and start to water. They'll get so heavy you'll want to close them to rest your eyes. When you close your eyes you'll feel your whole body getting tired and heavy, so tired that your arm will drop down onto your lap and you will go into a lovely comfortable sleep just listening to my voice. You may close your eyes any time while I'm counting, just as soon as they get tired and watery and then you go into that sleep all the sooner and I'll stop counting. Breathe in deeply and slowly now while I count.' A point of practical importance is that one should be prepared to catch the arm as it drops in case it hits the arm-rest of the dental chair.

7. *Relaxation through the Release of Tension*

This method well described in *The Practical Application of Medical and Dental Hypnosis* may be used with advantage on subjects who have failed to go into hypnosis by other means. In effect the subject arranges his own hypnosis.

It is a closed-eye technique in which the subject either sits in the dental chair with the feet flat on the foot-rest or in a chair with the feet flat on the floor, hands on lap with the palms down on legs above the knees. One proceeds:

'I want you to press down on your right knee very firmly, very firmly indeed, so hard that you will eventually feel that you will be able to push your foot through the floor [or foot-rest], so hard that when I try to lift your hand from your leg I will not be able to do so; if I can you are not pushing hard enough. That's fine! Keep it up! Keep up that rigidity—push and maintain it! Push harder, harder, harder!

'Now I want you to pay attention very carefully to what I am telling you. I want you to keep that pressure up until I count to three and at the count of three suddenly let go of that pressure and as you do so you experience a feeling of lightness in your hand and it starts to slide forward on your leg—as it slides forward it straightens at the elbow and as your arm straightens it leaves your leg altogether and it starts to rise higher and higher, higher and higher until it is parallel to the floor at shoulder height and then it stops. So at the count of three you just let go of all that pressure and your hand slides forward and your arm straightens and a feeling of lightness comes into it and it rises up into the air. ONE, TWO, THREE! Let go that tension! Your hand is sliding forward on your leg and as it slides it is straightening at the elbow. That's fine! and as your arm straightens it goes up, up, up, lifting, lifting, lifting, your whole arm begins to feel light, light as a feather, it rises up as though a balloon were tied to your wrist. Very good! higher and higher until it is parallel to the ground. That's fine! Now your arm will stay there—now I want you to let your arm get stiff and rigid from your shoulder, down through your elbow to your wrist and right through to your finger-tips so that your whole arm and hand and fingers feel stiff and rigid like a poker, like a bar of iron; so stiff and rigid that I could not bend it if I tried. You have made your arm so stiff and rigid that it just will not bend.' It may be noted in this particular wording that the subject has *not* been directly challenged, the challenge has been switched to the operator and he will be the judge as to the extent he will push the claim. When the initial suggestions of stiffness and rigidity are given to the subject the operator's hand may be lightly run down from the shoulder to the finger-tips once or twice and the incipient stiffness will be apparent.

Secter deepens the trance in the following manner:

'Now pay attention to the back of your arm as you keep it stiff and rigid . . . imagine I placed a couple of shopping bags there, each bag has about 20 lb of groceries. You realise and feel the weight of it and that weight keeps pushing your stiff and solid arm back to where it was before, pushing your leg down on to the floor. You try to keep your arm up but you just find it too much for you and soon your stiff and solid arm is back on your knee where the extra weight of the shopping bags helps to push down further on your knee. That's fine! Push, push, push, harder, harder, harder. Very good! I try to take your hand off but I can't . . . keep it up. Now I'm going to count slowly from one to three and at the count of three, let go quickly and melt into the chair, as quickly as a stretched-out rubber band collapses when it's let go, just like that and you go deeply relaxed. ONE, TWO, THREE! Deeply relaxed, breathe slowly and deeply.'

A propos this method Secter remarks: 'All these people have previously failed to go into hypnosis because people wanted to hypnotise them. *It is much easier to go into hypnosis if you know what to do and you do it yourself.*'

8. *Relative Analgesia used for the Hypnotic Induction of Completely Resistant Patients*

The following account is taken from Langa's *Relative Analgesia in Dental Practice*[3] and should be of considerable interest to all students of hypnosis.

'Bleadon and Sugarman had experienced the hypnotic trance countless times and thus when they were exposed to relative analgesia they were struck by the similarity of sensations. They set about investigating the effects of utilising hypnotic induction techniques on themselves while in a state of analgesia. The results were spectacular. Hypnotic induction was brought about almost immediately. A euphoric state with diminution of conscious awareness and muscular relaxation in excess of the degree usually obtainable with relative analgesia was evidenced. And this was brought about in thirty seconds. The nitrous oxide was then turned off and the investigators breathed only oxygen and air while the usual hypnotic induction procedure continued. Each investigator remained in a hypnotic trance deeper than he had ever experienced before and remained so until given the signal to come out. The decision was made to try this approach on resistant patients with whom they had failed repeatedly with the usual hypnotic techniques. It was found that *deep trances* could now be induced in these patients as *quickly as in good hypnotic subjects*. Post-hypnotic suggestion was then utilised: the subjects were told that subsequently they would go into a trance with the usual induction methods. This was also highly successful.'

One patient on being questioned offered the following information: 'I always had my mind wandering with many thoughts but with the combination of this gas with hypnosis I became completely calm, and my attention was completely fixed on your conversation.'

Ten resistant subjects in whom no demonstrable hypnosis could be obtained tried this approach and all were easily induced into a deep trance with the aid of relative analgesia.

Langa comments on these results by saying that hypnosis has become useful in dentistry as an aid in eliminating fear and anxiety. In this regard the use of nitrous oxide as relative analgesia not only eliminates the long induction period in almost all cases but it also makes it possible *to obtain hypnosis in almost every case.*

The writer would only disagree on one point with what has been said as *some* hypnotic induction techniques may be quite short as will be shown in the last method to be described. But here obviously is a field of considerable interest and importance in which two facts of clinical significance are at once apparent. Firstly, that all subjects will readily reach a deep stage of hypnosis and secondly, that the percentage of failures is apparently minimal.

The use of relative analgesia is steadily growing in this country insofar as dentistry is concerned, and it would seem that with these two modalities to hand the dental surgeon has two of the most valuable adjuncts that conservative dentistry has experienced in recent years.

Those dentists who do not wish to use relative analgesia may in future well be able to send patients resistant to hypnotic induction to a colleague who does use it for the initial trance induction.

Readers who have personally experienced the state of relative analgesia and of hypnosis will know very well the subjective similarity of these two conditions.

9. *Eye Closure* (*after Elman*)

Dave Elman[4] who died several years ago was neither a doctor nor a dentist, neither a professional psychologist nor a psychiatrist, but he taught thousands of doctors and dentists throughout America the art of hypnosis, particularly induction and deepening techniques.

His book *Explorations in Hypnosis* published in 1968 after his death is, to use a somewhat hackneyed phrase, a veritable mine of information and of immense practical value. It was Elman's prime contention that the initial stages of hypnotic procedure as currently taught were far too time-consuming and could be considerably shortened with immense advantage to the busy medical or dental practitioner. In this he undoubtedly succeeded as any operator-hypnotist who has faithfully followed his teaching well knows. It is indeed unfortunate that his book is no longer obtainable.

What follows is a description of his *Eye Closure Induction Technique* which is quick, simple and remarkably effective—later in this book equally effective deepening methods patterned after Elman will also be described:

'Take a long deep breath and close your eyes . . . now let those muscles round your eyes relax to the point where they won't work. . . . Test them and make sure they won't work . . . test them hard . . . that's right! that's very good! Now just let that feeling of relaxation go right down to your toes . . . that's fine. Now we'll do that exercise all over again but the next time I ask you to open and close your eyes that lovely feeling of relaxation will be twice as deep as it is now . . . twice as deep . . . you just let it be like that. Now open your eyes and really let yourself relax, . . . close your eyes again . . . that's it, very good indeed! and the next time you do this you'll relax even more . . . open your eyes . . . now close your eyes and experience the wave of relaxation that surges over you . . . now I'm going to lift your hand up and let it drop back into your lap . . . I want it to be as limp as a dish-rag . . . as limp as a rag doll. If you've followed your instructions properly, that relaxation will have gone right down to your toes. . . . And when I lift your hand up and let it go, it will flop down onto your lap, just let it flop down. . . . That's right . . . now you feel very, very relaxed, physically more relaxed than you've ever been.'

In order to conserve time Elman goes straight on from here with a deepening technique:

'Now I want you to make your mind as relaxed as your body is, so when I tell you I want you to start counting out *aloud backwards* from one hundred. Each time that you say a number you will *double your relaxation* and so by the time you get to 98 or 97 you will be so relaxed that the numbers won't be there any more. Start from 100 and watch them disappear before you get to 98 or 97 . . . double your relaxation and watch them start fading . . . now watch them disappear. . . . Now they'll be gone . . . *even as I lift your arm up and let it drop down onto your lap, so the numbers drop right out of your mind* . . . isn't that a nice feeling? Are they all gone? Let them disappear. . . . Are they all gone? That's right.'

The coupling of a motor activity with an effect that you wish to take place will be noted in the above exercise; 'even as I lift your arm up and let it drop down onto your lap, so the numbers drop out of your mind'. This is a very successful method of increasing a desired effect.

In the foregoing induction techniques it is impossible to state dogmatically that any one is better than the other: obviously the use of relative analgesia is a special case, but of the others, some are more time-consuming; Elman's eye closure is probably the quickest and enjoys a very high percentage of success. But successful induction does not however, in the writer's opinion, depend so much on what method is used as on the operator who uses it. Operators have, as indeed we all have, preferences and an operator who does not 'feel at home' with a particular method will very often fail. It is essential to familiarise oneself with more than one technique and this may be very easily brought about by using a different induction on the patient's second visit. You have given him a post-hypnotic signal for future induction on his first visit and, if you are wise, you will have put him back into hypnosis by means of this signal before he leaves your surgery (see p. 57). Now on this second visit you may use another induction technique telling him, in all truth, that you have another method of showing him how to relax and that this will result in a much deeper relaxed state—this is a very useful way of gaining confidence and of acquiring familiarity with the various ways of inducing hypnosis, particularly as failure is *very* unlikely in a subject who has already gone into hypnosis.

In this way it is possible to gain considerable experience in induction techniques with only a small number of patients. Now what are the mechanisms involved in these inductions? Bernard Gindes in his book *New Concepts of Hypnosis*,[5] in a chapter entitled 'The Mechanisms of Hypnosis', goes so far as to give a *Hypnotic Formula*, stating categorically that if it be meticulously carried out hypnosis *must* follow. As it is important for the operator-hypnotist to understand what he is actually doing in trying to reach his goal, the relevant part of Gindes' chapter is reproduced here:

MISDIRECTED ATTENTION + BELIEF + EXPECTATION = HYPNOSIS.

1. *Misdirected attention*: it is essential that the subject concentrate his attention upon something irrelevant to the actual hypnosis; his mind, focused on a diverting channel, becomes unable to harbour doubt.

2. *Belief*: the prime requisite of effective hypnosis is the belief of the subject in both the competence and integrity of the hypnotist. He must believe that the therapist can do what he has promised; he must believe in hypnosis as an acutal phenomenon; and he must believe in the inevitability of his personal surrender.

3. *Expectation*: with belief as a starting point, the subject must be conditioned to expectation. One suggestion works; the subject expects the next to take effect. When he expects to go to sleep, he will go to sleep and not before.

4. *Imagination*: imagination is the integrating factor which welds belief and expectation into an irresistible force.

Thus informed it may easily be realised that the methods of induction are truly legion!

In view of the 'welding' of belief and expectation by the subject's own imagination the writer would, *pace* Bernard Gindes, revise his formula graphically so that it reads:

MISDIRECTED ATTENTION + BELIEF + EXPECTATION
+ SUBJECT'S IMAGINATION = HYPNOSIS.

REFERENCES

1. WOLBERG, Lewis. *Medical Hypnosis*. Volume 1. Grune & Stratton, London & New York, 1948.
2. SHAW, Irwin S. *Clinical Applications of Hypnosis in Dentistry*. W. B. Saunders, London, 1958.
3. LANGA, Harry. *Relative Analgesia in Dental Practice*. W. B. Saunders, London, 1968.

4. ELMAN, Dave. *Explorations in Hypnosis*. Nash Publishing, Los Angeles, 1970.
5. GINDES, Bernard. *New Concepts in Hypnosis*. Allen & Unwin, London, 1953.

CHAPTER 4

The Phenomena of Hypnosis

It is not intended in a short practical treatise of this nature to delve deeply into all the phenomena that comprise the hypnotic spectrum, but a knowledge of some is mandatory if the dental surgeon intends to use hypnosis in general practice.

It will be appreciated that the manifestations of hypnotic phenomena cannot be divided up into watertight compartments; the hypnotic situation is a dynamic one in which fluctuations in depth occur from time to time, but for convenience they may be divided as here:

1. *The Hypnoidal State*

The subject sits in the chair in an obvious state of extreme relaxation with closed eyes and all the appearance of sleep but if the most simple post-hypnotic suggestion is given to him it will almost certainly not be carried out.

2. *The Light Trance*

The breathing becomes slower and deeper and there is catalepsy of the eyes. The subject exhibits a marked degree of lassitude with a disinclination to move or speak; rapport is strengthened and simple post-hypnotic suggestions will be carried out.

Glove analgesia may sometimes be effected, and as the relaxation secured is appreciable dental treatment which might otherwise cause resentment may be carried out to the satisfaction of both parties.

3. *The Medium Trance*

An interesting feature of the medium trance is that the subject if asked will usually acknowledge that he is in that condition.

Amnesia, at least partial, is usually but not always present and glove analgesia is readily produced in suitable subjects: the degree of analgesia present at this trance depth will permit conservative treatment without 'locals' in most cases.

4. *The Deep or Somnambulistic Trance*

The ability to open the eyes and not come out of the trance is said to be characteristic of the true somnambule: the writer would not agree and would say that the true test of somnambulism is the production of post-hypnotic positive and negative hallucinations.

Anaesthesia is complete, permitting all forms of dental treatment and generally amnesia is a normal concomitant.

The subject may be regressed in age and past memories may be recalled. The subject may also be told that he will experience a dream that will reveal specific troubles to him and that he will remember it later for discussion (an example of such a dream is given in the case histories, *see* p. 82).

Now to deal in a little more detail with the more important phenomena.

Relaxation

Even in the light trance muscular relaxation is very noticeable. The subject's hands are seen to be lying on his lap, the fingers usually slightly flexed. Both hands and fingers may remain motionless for long periods of time: if the arm be raised up by the sleeve the complete absence of tension is at once apparent, the arm being limp like that of a rag doll and on release it drops back onto the lap with a flop. The facial expression is invariably a relaxed one, the eyes being closed, although in the initial stages there may be some fluttering of the eyelids which later, but not always, ceases. Some degree of lachrymation is usually evident. The breathing becomes regular and shallow.

Increased Suggestibility

Possibly the most characteristic feature of hypnosis is a greatly increased suggestibility coupled with a by-passing of the critical faculty—in fact Elman gives a very good general definition of hypnosis when he states: '*Hypnosis is a state of mind in which the critical faculty of the human is by-passed and selective thinking established.'*

Suggestibility varies naturally with the type of suggestion; if, for example, a subject in a light trance is given the suggestion that he is seeing himself indulging in his favourite sport then, with very little reinforcement, he will soon begin to hallucinate the scene, but it will usually require a deeper state to secure analgesia of, say, the hand or some other part of the body.

Alterations in Muscular Activity

If the arm of a hypnotised subject is stretched out in front of him or raised above his head it will remain in that position indefinitely—a condition known as *Catalepsy*.

Both arms may be stretched out horizontally and the operator may initiate the rotation of the hands round and round—having started this movement it will continue automatically until the operator calls a halt: these *automatic movements* may incidentally be used as an excellent deepening technique.

Hypnotic Rapport

This may be defined as that relationship which is established between hypnotist and subject, in which the subject is highly sensitive to suggestions from the hypnotist, but insensitive to suggestions from any other source.

In this relationship the subject has a strong tendency to interpret the words of the hypnotist literally: for example, he is asked: 'Do you mind telling me your name?' and he replies: 'No', but interpreting the question literally he does not add his name. Hypnotic rapport is an important factor in successful hypnosis and its good establishment undoubtedly increases the subject's motivation to achieve his goal.

Sensory Phenomena

Any of the senses may be affected in hypnosis—for instance, the subject may be told that when he awakens from hypnosis he will notice an itch on the side of his nose and that he will feel compelled to rub his nose once or twice and the itch will go; on awakening he will perform this act. This may be taken as proof of hypnosis. In this connection it is important to remember that the itch experienced by the subject is identical in its final interpretation by him as that produced by a mechanical or organic cause. There is no such thing as imaginary pain, and *functional and organic pain* are *subjectively* similar.

Hallucinations, both positive and negative, may be produced in deep hypnosis.

A positive hallucination may be described as an experience having the character of sense perception, but without relevant or adequate sensory stimulation.

A negative hallucination is the failure to have perceptual experience when relevant and adequate stimuli are present.

Positive and negative hallucinations may be produced as the result of suggestions given to the subject in the trance and will, of course, be performed post-hypnotically; he may be told, for example, that when he wakes up a cat will come into the room and jump onto his lap, that he will stroke it once or twice and then it will jump down and go out of the room: this will happen exactly as predicted, and in a similar manner a subject may be told that a person sitting on a chair will no longer be there when he wakes up. In dentistry the manifestation of such bizarre effects seldom has a place, but it is of interest to note that in order to carry out the post-hypnotic suggestion the subject puts himself into hypnosis for the duration of the act.

The production of *Analgesia* is an important phenomenon and this will be dealt with later on in the book (p. 68).

Amnesia

Most, but not all, deep trance subjects develop a spontaneous amnesia on awakening; it may, however, be suggested in the lighter stages to 'encourage' the subject to forget any particularly difficult or painful passage during treatment. The writer feels very strongly that it is far better to train the patient adequately to accept all treatment with equanimity rather than to attempt to bury traumatic incidents in the subconscious to be the cause later for resentment; this point is perhaps debatable but it has been the writer's experience over many years that most problems, and they are fortunately few, encountered by the patient may be talked over at waking level and again in the hypnotic state *and be resolved.*

Regression

In psychotherapy regression may play a very important part: the subject may be regressed down the years to an age where a particular traumatic event took place and suitably dealt with. Obviously regression has a use in dental practice but unless the operator has considerable experience in dealing with any emotional involvement that may ensue, it would be wiser to avoid it, at least until he has gained that experience.

It is a vexed question to which it is difficult to give a definitive answer but it is sound advice to say:

1. Confine your hypnosis to your particular discipline, and

2. If you feel it necessary to use uncovering techniques, i.e. techniques in which you are uncovering latent material from the subconscious, then you *must* use a permissive approach which allows the subject to withhold traumatic incidents that he is not yet ready to give up: he is given what one may call an 'escape' clause. *The Ideo-motor Signalling Method* (p. 67) is ideal as the subject may be given four signals—'Yes', 'No', 'I don't know' and 'I don't want to answer that question'. One may choose, say, the index and little finger of each hand for the signals. Cheek and LeCron in *Clinical Hypnotherapy* and Hartland in *Medical and Dental Hypnosis* discuss this fully in their respective volumes.

Post-hypnotic Suggestions

It is impossible to exaggerate the importance of this hypnotic phenomenon. A suggestion given in the trance state will, with certain exceptions, take effect after the subject has been awakened. From this premise it follows that:

a. The subject will re-enter hypnosis at any future time on being given suitable suggestions during the trance; he may be given the simplest of cues which he will act upon immediately with an enormous saving of time.

b. The teaching of *Auto-hypnosis* becomes almost a matter of routine, all that is necessary is to explain to the subject when in hypnosis that he himself may use the same suggestions as in *a above* to put himself into a trance. This is *fully* explained elsewhere in this book (p. 64).

c. Instructions may be given in the trance state to be carried out later for some therapeutic purpose: this is most effective.

A case of the writer will serve as an illustration. A young patient complained of 'sore and bleeding gums' in the premolar area on the left-hand side of his mouth. Questioning revealed that his mastication was almost entirely unilateral. Sometime earlier he had experienced severe pain in |E; he avoided eating on this side and it was quite a while before this tooth was removed. The unilateral mastication had become a habit pattern. A short talk at conscious level, explaining the reason and suggesting that he would remember when he picked up his knife and fork to eat on both sides was ineffectual after 2 weeks. He was put into hypnosis and the previous instructions repeated. At his very next meal these instructions were carried out and there was no relapse.

d. Ego-strengthening owes it success to the power of post-hypnotic suggestion; this is well seen in 'morale boosting' when the subject is confronted from time to time with a situation involving fear of failure. The fortifying suggestions come into the mind at just the right time to aid him/her.

e. In the same manner that a subject will carry out positive suggestions so will he accept negative suggestions, provided they are carefully worded and do not conflict with his ethical and moral standards. They are almost 100 per cent successful and the safeguarding 'barring-out' clause is a good example.

To finalise here—one may say that post-hypnotic suggestions that seem reasonable and compatible with the subject's ethical and moral code will usually be acted upon. Improper suggestions invariably result in total rejection and spontaneous awakening.

It should not be forgotten that there is a *compulsive urge* to carry out a suggestion and if, for one reason or another, the subject has failed to carry it out, he should be put back into hypnosis and told he need no longer comply. In this way any anxiety caused by the inner conflict will be removed.

Deepening the Hypnotic Trance

The number of ways of deepening the hypnotic trance is truly legion: in a book of this nature it is proposed to describe only a selection that will prove practical in the dental chair. In deepening the hypnotic trance we are aiming at securing an appreciable degree of both physical *and* mental relaxation; now in the initial stage we have probably only succeeded in securing a reasonable degree of physical relaxation with very little mental relaxation.

Broadly speaking it is true to say that any action, any exercise that is successfully carried out by the subject will result in a deepening of the trance state; talking to him and suggesting that he relaxes more and more with each breath that he takes, synchronising your words with his own breathing—'. . . as you breathe *out* so you will feel yourself going down deeper and deeper into a more and more relaxed state'.

The effect of a series of relaxing exercises in hypnosis is cumulative and it is in the *compounding of suggestions* that depth may be obtained. The subject has accepted one simple suggestion, he is then presented with another perhaps more difficult one; his acceptance of the first has accomplished two things: (1) a deepening of the hypnosis and (2) a lowering of the critical faculty. The initial success of the first exercise has conditioned him to accept the next task and so, as each stage is successful, he becomes less and less critical and more and more ready to comply with any request. For example, in the production of analgesia in the mouth: it has been found that a greater depth is manifest when the analgesia is first demonstrated in the hand and then transferred to the tooth area by the subject. You have been *compounding suggestions and the effect is cumulative.* In the language of metaphor, you have heaped Ossa upon Pelion.

Before going on to describe some deepening exercises it will not come amiss to discuss briefly the advantages of depth. It has been rightly said that it is not always necessary to secure a deep trance in order to bring about the desired therapeutic goal and in dentistry a light stage of hypnosis will often permit conservative treatment that was previously impossible owing to the raised pain threshold which facilitates acceptance. But to obtain a definite analgesia in any area it is usually necessary to obtain a medium trance: it is unnecessary in these pages to stress the advantage of procuring analgesia in any desired area of the mouth; apart from the clinical gain the retention and demonstration of this phenomenon as a post-hypnotic suggestion leave the subject in no doubt whatsoever as to the validity of the hypnotic situation and as to his own ability to attain his desired goal, whatever that may be.

It is, however, in the *somnambule* that the value of deep hypnosis is seen to the best advantage: operative procedure is virtually a matter of routine and analgesia a normal concomitant. Esdaile (p. 3) who performed so many operations in India never suggested anaesthesia, his subjects simply being put into the deepest possible trance and successfully operated on.

Now for a more detailed description of deepening methods.

1. *Breathing Exercises*

These have already been briefly touched upon: Hartland in his book gives one of the best accounts of this simple but very effective method. In Chapter 8, p. 76, para. 3, he explains to the subject in the waking state *why* his depth will increase. 'Although none of us normally realises it, each time we breathe out in everyday life we tend to relax. Perhaps you would like to try this for yourself. Take a deep breath . . . fill your chest . . . and hold it until I tell you to let go. Notice the tension in your chest muscles . . . the tension in your shoulders and upper arms. And I want you to pay particular attention to how . . . the moment I say: "Let go!" . . . all that tension disappears immediately . . . and you tend to sag limply down into the chair. Now . . . LET GO!'

Hartland then uses a combined breathing and counting method in which the subject is told that as the operator counts slowly from one to five he will take five very deep breaths, and that each time he breathes out—slowly and deliberately—he will feel himself becoming more and more deeply relaxed. 'ONE . . . deep, deep breath . . . more and more deeply relaxed . . . deeper and deeper asleep' and so on up to five.

This is followed by one final exercise in breathing as follows: 'I want you to take one *very deep breath* . . . fill your chest . . . and hold it until I say: "Let go!" and as you do, let your breath out *as quickly as possible* and you feel yourself sagging limply back into the chair . . . and you will become twice as deeply relaxed as you are now . . . twice as deeply asleep. Now take that very deep breath . . . fill your chest . . . HOLD IT! . . . hold it as long as you can and then LET GO . . . and feel how you melt down into the chair deeply relaxed.'

The wording has been slightly altered here as Hartland himself tells the subject when to relax and let go, and he usually waits 50–60 seconds: the writer opines that the ability to hold the breath for any length of time is very much an individual factor and leaves it to the subject to decide.

2. *Loss of Numbers* (*after Dave Elman*)

This very good method has already been described as a follow-on from Elman's eye-closure technique but it may equally well follow any other initial induction.

3. *Limb Rigidity*

The subject's arm is stretched out horizontally at shoulder level and he is asked to concentrate his thoughts upon his arm.

'I am going to stroke your arm from the shoulder down to the tips of your fingers and with each stroke I shall count out aloud from one to five. Your arm will get stiffer and stiffer with each count so that by the time I reach five it will have become so stiff that it will feel like an iron bar, a steel poker and *I will be quite unable to bend it.*

'ONE! your arm is beginning to feel stiff, like a poker, like a bar of iron.

'TWO! the stiffness increases and it is beginning to feel as though you had no joints, just a solid poker.

'THREE! the stiffness is going right down to your wrist and soon it will reach your fingers, the very tips of your fingers.

'FOUR! your whole arm and your hand right down to your finger-tips seem just like a solid bar, a steel poker.

'FIVE! Your arm, your hand right down to your finger-tips now feel like one solid steel bar and although I try to bend it, I am quite unable to do so . . . the more I try the more rigid it becomes. . . . In a moment or two I am going to count slowly backwards from three to one and at one all the stiffness, all the rigidity will leave your arm and it will sink down onto your lap; even as it drops down so you will drop down into a deeper and deeper relaxed state.

'THREE! the stiffness is beginning to leave your fingers and your arm.

'TWO! your arm is losing all its rigidity, all its stiffness.

'ONE! all the stiffness and tension have gone and when I take my hand from under your arm it will drop down with a flop onto your lap and you go down deeper and deeper into a lovely relaxed state.'

The operator is able in this exercise to judge the extent of the rigidity as he is stroking the arm down from the shoulder and he should be reasonably certain when he gives the indirect challenge that it will succeed: it may be noted that the challenge is indirect insofar as the subject is *not* challenged, only the operator testing the rigidity.

4. *Automatic Movements*

Two exercises will be described here; both are equally effective.

a. Arm movement—the subject's arm is placed upon the arm of the chair, the forearm is raised to the vertical position, being grasped at the wrist by the operator and with the elbow forming the pivotal point the forearm is moved slowly forwards and backwards.

'Your arm goes slowly backwards and forwards . . . backwards and forwards . . . imagine a piece of cord looped around your wrist and someone at each end of the cord is pulling your arm . . . backwards . . . then forwards.

'Just picture that piece of cord, tied round your wrist. Think very hard about it, get it firmly fixed in your mind as your arm is being slowly pulled . . . backwards and . . . forwards. When I let go of your wrist in a few moments it will feel as though that cord is still there pulling your arm backwards . . . and forwards and so your arm will go on moving all on its own backwards . . . and forwards. You don't try to make it move, you don't try to stop it, you just let it happen. It just goes on automatically . . . backwards . . . and forwards . . . backwards and forwards . . . until I ask you to stop.' The wrist is released and the arm continues to move automatically. 'Stop! let your arm drop back down onto your lap and as it does so you relax deeper and deeper, very, very deeply relaxed.'

b. Hand and wrist rotation—the hands and forearms are stretched out horizontally in front of the subject with the elbows bent and the hands are rotated around each other in a circular movement; the subject is told that when you release his wrists they will continue the rotation of his hands until asked to stop when they will drop down onto his lap etc.

5. *The Descending Lift or Elevator*

There are one or two versions of this deepening technique. A wise precaution before using this method is to make certain that the subject is not suffering from a lift phobia; in such cases an *escalator* may often be successfully substituted. Hartland describes his method in which the operator or therapist accompanies the subject in his descent; it is claimed that this materially increases the effectiveness of the exercise.

'Please imagine we are standing together on the fifth floor of a large department store . . . we are about to step into the lift to descend to street level. As we go down and the lift gates open and close and people get in and others get out so you become deeper and deeper relaxed, all the time deeper and deeper relaxed. We step into the lift, the gates close and we sink slowly downwards.

'The lift stops at the *fourth floor* . . . several people get out . . . two more get in . . . the gates close again . . . already you are becoming more and more deeply relaxed . . . more and more deeply asleep. And as we sink down to the *third floor* . . . and stop whilst the gates open and close again . . . you are relaxing more and more, all the time more and more, deeper and deeper asleep. Slowly down to the *second floor* . . . one or two people get out and several get in . . . and as they do so . . . you are feeling much more deeply relaxed, much more deeply asleep. Now down once again to the *first floor* . . . the gates open and close . . . but nobody gets out and nobody gets in. Already you have become more deeply relaxed . . . still more deeply asleep. Deeper and deeper asleep.

'We go down yet further . . . until at last the lift stops at *street level*. The gates open . . . and everybody gets out. *But we do not get out.*

'We decide to go down still deeper . . . and so we descend to the basement. The lift gates close again . . . and down, down we go . . . down and down . . . deeper and deeper . . . and when we arrive at the basement . . . you are feeling twice as deeply relaxed . . . very, very comfortably relaxed . . . twice as deeply asleep.'

Hartland points out that the total unexpectedness of this last stage, the journey to the basement, comes as a surprise to the subject and results in even greater depth.

6. *Fractionation* (*after Vogt*)

Basically fractionation consists in putting the subject into hypnosis and bringing him out of it again in rapid succession; it is said that with each re-induction he goes into a deeper and deeper state of hypnosis. This may be very noticeable, the subject after four or even five re-inductions often showing considerable reluctance to come out of hypnosis.

Apart from the rapid induction and re-induction method of fractionation a more subtle method attributed to André M. Weitzenhoffer which the writer has used on many occasions will be briefly described; that this results in an appreciable increase in depth is well confirmed by subjective elicitation.

With the subject in hypnosis one proceeds:

'In a few moments I am going to ask you to wake up. I shall start counting slowly backwards from *five to one*, and at *one* you will open your eyes and wake up, very pleased with the way you have been able to relax, very pleased indeed. Then I shall be talking to you and you will notice that, although I am speaking to you and you are trying to listen to me, you will begin to feel very tired and sleepy and you will have great difficulty in keeping your eyes open, your eyelids become so heavy, so very heavy that you feel you must close them and you just feel you cannot concentrate any longer and you close your eyes letting yourself sink back down into the chair experiencing the most wonderful relaxation you have ever had.'

As with most hypnotic instructions this may be repeated with advantage.

CHAPTER 5

The Practical Application of Hypnosis

Chairside Hypnosis

THE presentation of hypnosis to the patient, the dangers, uses and abuses, the limitations, induction techniques and deepening have all been discussed in these pages.

Auto-hypnosis and auto-analgesia alone remain but these two very important hypnotic phenomena will be fully explained in the next chapter; the time, it is thought, is now ripe to explain fully the implementation of hypnosis in dental treatment. It has been wisely said that it is relatively easy to induce the hypnotic trance in a large proportion of patients, especially dental patients; this is almost certainly due to the high motivational factor that prevails as dental subjects have nearly always everything to gain and nothing to lose in achieving total relaxation; it is seldom, if ever, that we are uncovering latent material that the subject is unwilling to reveal. What is not so easy is to know precisely how to take full advantage of the hypnotic trance when you have got it. Let us assume that you have a patient in the chair who has just gone into hypnosis; you have, I hope, told him, be he young or adult, that you are only going to teach him to relax at this visit and that no treatment will be carried out; this is, I believe, not always current teaching but I think it is important as it at once removes any fear that treatment will be commenced against the subject's will and thereby greatly facilitates the induction.

As the treatment of the adult differs somewhat from the young boy or girl, in that the 'training' may be shortened, we will take the case of an adult first.

Initially the trance may be quickly deepened by simple breathing exercises (p. 50) and then a further deepening such as Elman's counting backwards with loss of numbers (p. 39) may be employed; this is very effective in most patients and not very time-consuming. If the operator is not happy with this technique then arm rigidity or automatic arm movements may be resorted to; these have been fully described elsewhere under deepening (p. 50). It is well to point out at this juncture that the operator is far more likely to succeed in hypnotic procedure if he makes use of a method that he himself has confidence in and with which he is completely familiar; lack of confidence is very readily communicated to the patient.

At this stage I would teach the patient acceptance of his treatment somewhat after the following manner:

'Your mind is now relaxed as well as your body, it is a very pleasant feeling indeed and now that you have learned to relax so well I want to show you how you can use this to further your treatment, to make your dental treatment easy and more than tolerable for you. Because you are now so relaxed things that previously worried you will no longer have any effect on you at all, and you will be very very pleased about it. Now I want you to open your mouth please and to keep it wide open; you'll find it very easy to do that now you are so relaxed . . . thank you . . . in a moment or two I am going to turn the high-speed drill on and you will notice the high-pitched whine, and I will start slowly counting from *one to ten* and as I do so the sound seems to get less and less noticeable until at *ten* it doesn't trouble you at all, although, of course, you will always hear it.' All the time the handpiece is brought *nearer and nearer* until it is close to the face. 'I am just going to put the saliva ejector in your mouth to keep it dry, you will hear the slight gurgling noise that it makes but it doesn't bother you in the least. Now I am putting the drill in your mouth and am going to turn it on with the water spray but of course the saliva ejector will take care of that. But nothing will be done today, you have been promised; you will realise now you have learned to relax how nice it is and will be for you to sit there calm and contented while you are having your dental work done.'

It would, of course, be possible to commence treatment at this stage but, on the whole, *even if permission has been obtained from the patient, as indeed it must be*, I would prefer to defer it until the next visit. The operator would do well to remember that a word of praise, of congratulation on the patient's progress never comes amiss. 'You have done very well indeed and the next time you come you will be able to relax quickly and into an even deeper state. I want you to listen carefully to what I am telling you: on your next visit, when you sit in the chair you will look down at your hands which are lying along the length of your thighs and I will count from *one to five* and at *five* your eyes will close and you will sink down into the chair just as relaxed as you are now, even more so.' These instructions are repeated slowly twice and then the patient is asked *to wake himself up* as follows: ' Soon I am going to ask you to wake yourself up, and you do this by counting out aloud from *five to one* and at *one* you open your eyes and wake up very pleased with your experience, very pleased indeed. Remember you will be able to go back into this very pleasant relaxed state in the chair by just looking down at your hands while I count from *one to five* and at *five* your eyes are closed and you are deeply relaxed.'

After a brief discussion with the patient about his feelings under hypnosis, you will, if you are wise, re-induce hypnosis by the prearranged post-hypnotic signal. This is very satisfactory for the operator and also serves to convince the subject of the validity of the hypnotic situation.

Earlier in this chapter the high-speed drill was introduced to the patient and this, what I call for want of better words, weapon of offence was brought to the patient's notice and even used to deepen the trance; take the saliva ejector or indeed the aspirator. You may say: 'As you sit there calm and relaxed just listening to my voice and the slight noise of the saliva ejector in your mouth so you relax deeper and deeper.' It is the writer's contention that the *second visit* is the all-important one: it is true that there are very quick methods of hypnotic induction available followed by equally rapid deepening techniques and that these methods are successful in a large number of cases, for example Dave Elman's eye-closure method of induction followed by the loss of numbers. These have been previously described, but if you are going to teach the patient auto-hypnosis, and possibly auto-analgesia, explain the significance of the barring-out clause and include even a modified version of Hartland's ego-strengthening and all this in one visit, you will be making heavy inroads into the available time in a busy practice.

The writer would emphasise that, apart from auto-analgesia, which may or may not always be necessary and which you may or may not always be able to produce, *the rest is obligatory. It is the aim of the operator, or should be, to teach the patient independence; he has been taught what to do and he is confident of his own ability to do it.*

In using hypnosis as an adjunct in dental treatment the dental surgeon accepts definite responsibility and he must fully appreciate the delicate balance that exists between the conscious and subconscious mind. The chapter that follows on auto-hypnosis and auto-analgesia makes this and other points abundantly clear. Now on this second visit no time need be wasted in obtaining hypnosis and a rapid deepening may be procured by one or other of the standard methods, for example automatic hand or arm movements, well described in Hartland's *Medical and Dental Hypnosis*—a point of practical application here is to have the subject open his eyes for a short time and look at his hands going round and round or his arm going backwards and forwards. 'In a moment or two I want you to open your eyes and just look at your hands as they go round and round, just automatically round and round, and then I shall ask you to close them again and as you do so you will notice a wave of relaxation that surges over you and you become more deeply relaxed than ever.' This is a very good way to increase depth.

Conservative treatment may well be started at this stage: many practitioners have said that this is the time when they suffer most from lack of confidence and even embarrassment. This need not be so and is, indeed, quite unnecessary, as all dental surgeons are, to be sure, very capable of reassuring and encouraging their patients in the normal course of treatment. In hypnosis they may do just the same, the fact that you have by-passed the critical faculty and established selective thinking makes them very ready to listen to your words. You may explain to the patient what you are doing at any stage, particularly if it be something unusual and you may ask him for his co-operation if you need it, although in the normal course of events the only co-operation you require of him is a passive one. You may reassure him from time to time with words such as: 'Now that you are sitting there so relaxed and calm, nothing that I have to do for you will worry you in the least, you accept it all quite willingly and you are very pleased about it. You are doing very well, very well indeed.'

If, during the treatment, he has let his mouth close a little the time-honoured dentist's phrase "A little wider, please!" is all that is required, *but* you will also remember if you are not working in the mouth for a while, to ask the patient to close it—muscles get tired.

Patients can open their eyes in hypnosis and remain in a trance. You want the patient to rinse his mouth out? all right, you say: 'In a minute or so I am going to ask you to open your eyes and remain in the relaxed state you are now in; I want you to listen carefully to what I have to say. You may feel a little reluctant to open your eyes at first but you can if you try. I am going to count slowly from *one to three* and at *three* you will open your eyes but you will not wake up, you will not wake up and you will remain in the same wonderfully relaxed condition that you are now in: then I want you to lean over and take up the glass of pink mouthwash and rinse your mouth out once or twice and then put the glass down, close your eyes and lean your head back on the head-rest. As you close your eyes and lean your head back you will notice a wave of relaxation that sweeps over you and you feel more deeply relaxed than ever.'

A propos the preceding paragraph, some of the textbooks state that only somnambules can open their eyes and not wake up: if this be so then the writer can claim a very large number amongst the patients he has trained! Perhaps some patients do come out of hypnosis if they open their eyes; the point is a purely academic one as, having accepted the operator's suggestion that they will close their eyes, lean back in the chair and be deeply relaxed, they carry it out to the letter. The question is raised here because the impression has been gained by some inexperienced operators that should the subject come out of hypnosis at this stage difficulty will be experienced in re-entry. This may be categorically denied and in many years of practice the writer has never encountered any anxiety in this respect.

Undoubtedly most subjects remain in hypnosis—the complete look of dissociation and the slow purposeful way that the glass is picked up and put down proves this point. The few who do come out of hypnosis will accept your suggestion as a post-hypnotic signal for re-induction.

It is not suggested that you keep up a conversation or a running commentary with your patients—they are reluctant to talk in hypnosis in any case and all you need do is occasionally to put in a word or two. Do not forget that there is no hurry in hypnosis, the patient is quite happy to sit there as long as you require, even longer!

It may happen that you wish to leave the patient alone for a few minutes—that urgent phone call, that cup of coffee that one never seems to have time to drink! So long as you tell him it does not matter in the least, otherwise he may well find himself out of touch and could possibly come out of hypnosis. Your short absence may be used to deepen the trance still more, you may say: 'I have to leave you alone for a few minutes, perhaps four or five, but it will not worry you in the least, you can sit there deeply relaxed and contented; perhaps you might like to think of some calm relaxing scene, a warm sunny day by the coast, a walk in the country or sitting by a lake in the mountains, the choice is yours, you choose the most pleasant calm relaxed scene you can think of, let yourself get really involved in it, enjoy it to the full—when you have got it fixed in your mind, would you just raise the index finger of your right hand, your right hand, to let me know you have the picture and are enjoying it, please?' Here the index finger is gently stroked by the operator once or twice and after some seconds' interval the index finger rises up. 'That's very good! please put your finger down and just let yourself enjoy your picture to the full and when I speak to you again in a few minutes you will have become even more deeply relaxed.'

This is a very good and practical use of visual imagery and may be employed on many occasions, being particularly useful during the actual treatment. If this has been proceeding in a normal manner some form of visual imagery may be suggested to the patient with advantage. It is germane to the subject to point out here that you may, of course, 'break in' to his picture from time to time with any explanation you may require to give him.

Now a few words about indiscreet remarks—there can be no doubt that in the past some post-operative setbacks were iatrogenic in origin; it was for far too long assumed that an anaesthetised subject was quite incapable of appreciating remarks made during the course of an operation in the theatre. *Injudicious remarks made during the course of operations have been recovered verbatim from patients who have later been put into hypnosis.*

A deep-trance subject may well exhibit post-hypnotic amnesia, but derogatory remarks and the like may be repressed into the subconscious, later to become a cause for resentment. Apart from any actual harm that may be caused, this behaviour has always seemed to the writer to be unworthy of a healing profession: the precept 'The dignity of the subject is sacrosanct' fits in well here. Cheek and LeCron in their excellent *Clinical Hypnotherapy* have a very good chapter on this subject, which could be read to advantage by every dental surgeon who uses hypnosis or anaesthesia.

Finally, what is the procedure to adopt if difficulty is encountered during the course of treatment? The patient becomes restless; he shows signs of withdrawing away from the instrumentation. What are you to do? You may either bring him out of hypnosis and discuss the matter or take steps to deepen the existing trance state. On balance I much prefer the latter course which succeeds in the majority of cases; indeed it is a remarkable fact that one seldom meets with any serious difficulty in actual treatment if the patient has been carefully schooled initially. What the writer has called 'pre-treatment rehearsals' will pay handsome dividends. Even a peremptory perusal of the psychological literature will convince the student of the advantages to be gained by proper patient training. A point of some interest here is that Cheek and LeCron in discussing hypnosis and surgery say: 'Remember that the human mind is capable of *standing stimuli which are usually considered painful if you explain what you are going to do*, that there may be some discomfort but that this will be minimal when he follows your directions *exactly* as you give them.'

To return now to the patient—we have left him in the trance state but have, of course, called a halt to the actual treatment. One proceeds: 'I noticed you seemed a little worried just now, was it because your treatment proved more disturbing than you expected? Please nod your head if that is the case', a pause and the patient nods his head. 'I see! well I will show you how you can overcome this difficulty, how you can relax deeper and deeper, so much deeper that you will not be disturbed again: it is very simple, just listen carefully. I am going to start counting very slowly from *one to five*, at *one* you take a very deep breath and hold it as long as you reasonably can and then you *slowly* let it out, at *two* you repeat the process and so on; each time that you exhale you feel yourself going down into a deeper and deeper relaxed state. Now at *five* you take the deepest possible breath, hold until you can't hold it any longer and then let it out as *quickly* as you can and notice how you sink down into the chair with all the tension in your body released.' This simple repetitive exercise will be found most effective in all but the most stubborn cases.

The effect of repetition and reinforcement will often come as a surprise to the inexperienced operator.

Thus we have a method of overcoming difficulties which lies in reinforcing suggestions resulting in an increase of trance depth; this, in turn, effects a raising of the pain threshold.

Occasionally failures will be encountered but they will nearly always occur in patients who have not had local anaesthesia for their conservative treatment; now in practice one finds that a very large percentage of patients may be treated under hypnosis without 'locals' but the few who cannot may, of course, be offered a local anaesthetic.

The criticism has been offered that if local anaesthesia has to be used hypnosis is a failure. This is nonsense; every dentist has seen many, many patients who, although they will submit to treatment, do so with the greatest reluctance; despite the local injection they sit in the chair with every muscle tensed communicating their fears to the unfortunate operator. It is indeed a debatable point whether the operator is the more delighted when the session is terminated or the patient!

These same patients treated under hypnosis present a transformation that is truly wonderful to behold. They sit in the chair, eyes closed with muscles completely relaxed: on questioning they will readily tell you that all their fears have gone and indeed that they quite look forward to coming to the surgery now!

To sum up the situation, it may be fairly stated that provided the subject will go into hypnosis and further deepening exercises have been carried out together with 'pre-treatment rehearsals', the dental session will proceed in a normal and satisfactory manner in almost every case.

The production of auto-analgesia in those patients who are capable of learning it still further increases the percentage of success. Auto-analgesia is dealt with in the next chapter. Dental treatment has now been carried out under hypnosis, it remains for you to explain the barring-out clause, auto-hypnosis and ego-strengthening (preferably a shortened or modified form). Auto-analgesia may, if time is running short, be left for another visit, but if you do this you must *on no account* omit the safeguards connected specifically with it, for example the dangers inherent in masking organic pain.

CHAPTER 6

Auto-hypnosis and Auto-analgesia

To deal with auto-hypnosis firstly—it is the writer's unshakable conviction that the teaching of auto-hypnosis *must* accompany the use of hypnosis in dentistry. The reasons for this conviction will be made clear as this chapter develops. Now the application of hypnosis in dentistry differs somewhat from medicine. It is earnestly to be hoped that all our patients will present themselves regularly every six months for possible treatment and it is essential that they submit themselves readily and happily if treatment be necessary—essential that is, if we are to claim that hypnosis is a necessary and successful adjunct in dentistry. *The real criterion of success, however, lies in the ability of the patients to accept treatment by the original operator-hypnotist or any other operator of his choice*, and if this be not so, then we have failed them and the use of hypnosis may rightly be condemned.

Fortunately, correct auto-hypnotic training will result in a patient who is able to accept treatment from any operator of his choice, but this training does carry with it a considerable responsibility on the part of the dentist and there are safeguards *which you must on no account omit*; with this proviso in mind it may be said that auto-hypnosis will prove of inestimable benefit to the patient.

A moment of thought will make the necessity of releasing the patient from any dependency on any one operator obvious. Dentists have no claim to immortality, indeed, sad to relate, the records for longevity are somewhat depressing! also, of course, your patient for one reason or another may seek treatment elsewhere. It is therefore of paramount importance that he is able to fend for himself and that the rapport that has been established is so canalised by auto-hypnosis, and where possible auto-analgesia, that it has been transferred to the very subject himself. He has learned to stand on his own two feet as it were. The suggestibility that he once had for the operator has been passed over to him in the form of an auto-suggestibility. A serious charge has been laid at our door concerning the dangers of transference. *Transference* in psycho-analysis may be described as the development of an emotional attitude, positive or negative, love or hate, towards the analyst on the part of the patient or subject; this emotional attitude may, of course, be either of a homo- or heterosexual nature. A well-known lecturer once said that the degree of transference created in dentistry could be such that, however poor the standard of our work, patients would never leave us, they were ours for life! Fortunately, for all practical purposes we may dismiss this sweeping statement as having little or no foundation and it will be shown how the full implementation of auto-hypnosis leaves the subject or patient completely confident of his own ability to accept treatment.

If you have taught your patient auto-hypnosis, combined for good measure with ego-strengthening (p. 15), he should be able to cope virtually with any eventuality that may arise, because, in the main, you have given him the two most important factors, that is the "know-how" to submit willingly to all necessary operative procedures and with ego-strengthening the self-confidence that removes the final doubt.

In the final analysis *all hypnosis is auto-hypnosis* and it is because of this fact that the production of auto-hypnosis presents few if any problems. The subject goes into hypnosis because he wishes to do so; he is motivated towards success, particularly in dentistry and the role of the hypnotist ought to be regarded as that of teacher and guide and be entirely permissive. It may be categorically stated that if the subject will go into hypnosis, then he will just as easily go into hypnosis *for himself* provided that he knows what to do. Here is the *modus operandi*: 'In a minute or two I want you to wake yourself up and when you do so you will be very, very pleased with the way you have learned to relax so well, very pleased indeed. You will be able to wake yourself up when I ask you to by counting out aloud backwards from *five to one* and at *one* you will open your eyes and be fully awake—now you will be able to put yourself back into this deeply relaxed condition *always provided that the time is right and the place is right* by looking down at your hands which are lying in your lap and counting out aloud from *one to five* and with each count you will feel yourself relaxing more and more and the numbers will become fainter and fainter so that by the time you reach *five* you are scarcely able to say the number and your eyes close and your whole body sinks down deeply into the chair absolutely relaxed.' These instructions may be repeated with advantage and then a full explanation of the right time and place, the so-called *barring-out clause*, is given.

The writer considers auto-hypnosis obligatory in which case the barring-out clause is mandatory whether or not the patient is taught auto-analgesia. Confirmation from the patient that he understands and agrees with your instructions is obtained by *ideo-motor response* in the trance state.

The exact wording that you use to explain the barring-out clause may be left to you but it is important not to miss any of the salient points. My particular verbalism goes somewhat like this:

'In learning to relax for yourself I want to give you some instructions that are for your own good and that will safeguard your interests. I want you to listen to them very carefully so that there is no possibility of your misunderstanding them. Because of what you have learnt you can, in some measure, by means of your subconscious mind control your conscious actions: now it would be very wrong of you to demonstrate your ability to go into hypnosis to all and sundry, it is for you and you alone. Naturally you would willingly put yourself into hypnosis for a doctor, dentist or a psychiatrist who had cause to require it of you, and this would also include a demonstration at a scientific meeting but does *not under any circumstances include cocktail parties and the like*. These same limitations apply in allowing yourself to be hypnotised by another person.

'Now if you wanted to relax yourself you would always be able to do so, provided that the time and place were suitable. For example, at a time when you would normally be able to sit in an arm-chair, say after lunch, and have 20–30 minutes' rest. You may give yourself the suggestion that your period of relaxation will last for a definite time and that when you wake up you will do so feeling very refreshed and pleased with your achievement. You need have no fear that in the event of anything untoward happening you would not wake up. If the telephone rang *and you wished to answer it* you would immediately wake up, likewise the ringing of the front door bell would have the same effect.' Your barring-out clause is all-embracing and you include, if appropriate, the mother and her child. 'If your baby started to cry you would instantly wake up and attend to her.' *A final precaution*: 'In the unlikely event that there was a smell of burning you would again be instantly awake and ready to take action; you would in fact be more quickly aware of an emergency than if you were in a normal sleep but at the same time repetitive noises of an inconsequential nature would not worry you in the least.'

This just about covers every eventuality and every word of it may then be repeated, perhaps a little more quickly! Remember, repetition pays handsome dividends in hypnosis.

Finally, one obtains approval and understanding from the patient by means of *ideo-motor signalling*, it having been established that this form of confirmation is more conclusive than a purely verbal one:

'Now before I ask you to open your eyes and wake up I want you to let me know that you have completely understood the instructions you have just received and that you will never abuse the ability that you now have to relax so completely. I want you to signify that you understand and agree to abide by these instructions which are entirely for your own good by raising the index finger of your right hand, *just raise the index finger of your right hand* to tell me that you understand and agree.' There is usually a delay of a few seconds before the finger is raised somewhat jerkily in acquiescence. One may then proceed: 'That's good, very good indeed; in a moment or two you may wake yourself up by counting backwards aloud from *five to one* and at *one* you will open your eyes and be fully awake very pleased with your relaxation, very pleased indeed. You will be able to put yourself back into hypnosis simply by looking down at your hands which are lying in your lap and counting slowly out aloud from *one to five* and with each count you will feel yourself relaxing more and more and the numbers becoming fainter and fainter so that by the time you reach *five* you are scarcely able to say the number and your eyes close and you sink down into the chair deeply relaxed, very deeply relaxed indeed. I want you to wake yourself up now, please!' After discussing any small points with the subject one may then say:

'Well, now that you have learned to relax I want you to show me how well you can do it, please. You know exactly what you have to do and you know that failure is absolutely impossible, quite impossible, so just relax, please.'

Auto-analgesia

It has been said earlier that if the subject will go into hypnosis, then he will go into *hypnosis for himself* if he knows exactly what to do; it is purely a matter of teaching. Now exactly the same may be said about analgesia. If the subject has accepted your suggestion in hypnosis and has produced hypnotic analgesia in, say, the hand which has been retained and demonstrated as a post-hypnotic phenomenon, then the teaching of auto-analgesia also becomes a matter of routine.

Apart from the obvious value auto-analgesia serves a two-fold purpose.

1. It is a very good deepening exercise in itself.
2. It convinces the subject to an even greater extent of the validity of the hypnotic situation than anything else: the retention of analgesia in some definite area of the body as a post-hypnotic phenomenon presents him with a *fait accompli* that brooks no argument.

Most of the methods used in the production of analgesia for dental purposes involve two stages. Analgesia is, for example, demonstrated in the hand and then transferred to the mouth. One may well ask: Why not produce it in the first instance around the tooth? Why go to the trouble of obtaining analgesia of the hand or finger and transferring it ultimately to the desired area? It has been found as a result of much clinical experience that a more profound effect is noticed by adopting this seemingly roundabout procedure and it should not be forgotten that every exercise that is given to the subject and *successfully* carried out usually results in a deepening of the trance state. There is also the strong possibility that the subject may doubt, consciously or subconsciously, his ability to produce analgesia in his mouth, a particularly sensitive area, *but having successfully accomplished it in his hand his doubts are considerably lessened.*

In a perusal of the now extensive literature on the subject of hypnotic analgesia the impression is gained that it is one of the more difficult phenomena to demonstrate. John Hartland in *Medical and Dental Hypnosis* says that complete analgesia is obtained in approximately 20% of subjects and that this achievement is indicative of a deep or somnambulistic trance.

It has been the writer's experience, an experience that has been shared by some colleagues, that an *adequate* but not necessarily complete analgesia may be obtained in an appreciably larger percentage of purely dental subjects; *motivation* may here play a large part as, in the main, the dental patient has nothing to lose and everything to gain in achieving his goal. This undoubtedly accounts also for the high incidence of successful inductions in dental practice.

There are many ways of producing hypnotic analgesia: Wolberg in *Medical Hypnosis*, Volume 1, describes a very good method albeit somewhat lengthy. Firstly, he effects a *hyperaesthesia* of one hand and then follows this up with *analgesia* of the other. The writer has used his technique very many times and has found it to be most successful—the first part will be quoted more or less verbatim. Wolberg says: 'Imagine you are walking down a long corridor and at the end of the corridor in the corner there is a pail of hot water. You know the water is hot because of the steam that is rising from it. Now when you can see this in your mind I want you to indicate to me that you can see the pail by raising the left hand about six inches. Good! Now bring it down again. You become curious about how hot the water in the pail is, so you walk over to the pail, take your right hand and you plunge it into the water. As you do, see how vivid you can make this in your mind so that you feel the heat, the pain and the smarting in your hand. Your hand will tingle or feel warm and tender. When you feel this sensation, your left hand will rise about six inches to indicate this to me. Good! Now as you sit there I am going to touch your right hand with a pin and you will notice how very sensitive it has become, very different from the other hand which you scarcely notice at all.'

This is what Wolberg says but one may, of course, vary the wording to suit one's own personality. The writer would make one important variation in the wording and that concerns the hot water. A patient has come out of the trance spontaneously when asked to plunge the hand into hot water, the explanation being given, quite naturally that they were afraid of being scalded. Hartland has a word to say about this in his book. The explanation ought to be given to the subjects that the water in the pail is very hot but not nearly hot enough to scald them, they need have no fear of that, they can easily bear the temperature. This hyperaesthesia may be retained and demonstrated to the subjects post-hypnotically and they may then put themselves back into hynposis (still maintaining the hyperaesthesia in the right hand) and analgesia of the left hand may be produced by one or other method. Increased sensitivity has been produced by suggestions of heat so it would seen logical to effect the opposite by suggestions of extreme cold and this, indeed, is an excellent way. The writer verbalises his suggestions somewhat after the following manner: 'Now I want you to imagine you are back again in the long corridor—you have already plunged your right hand into the pail of hot water and your hand has become and remains very sensitive—just turn round and look at the wall opposite—there in the corner you see another pail, being curious about this pail you step over to it and look down at it: you notice that it is about three-quarters full of water but unlike the water in the other pail this water is very, very cold, ice-cold in fact. You take an even closer look and you see large chunks of ice floating in the water. Look carefully and nod your head to let me know you can see it—Good! Now you plunge your left hand right into the water and you notice how ice-cold it is, you keep your hand there for a little while. Your hand becomes very, very cold indeed, so cold that it feels quite numb with cold, it is quite without feeling, quite insensitive. The feeling is rather as though you had drawn a thick heavy leather glove right over your left hand, such a thick glove that you wouldn't expect to feel anything through it. You withdraw your hand from the ice-cold water; it feels quite numb with the cold. I am just going to touch your *right hand* with the pin again and of course you withdraw it smartly as it is so sensitive. There you see! But your *left hand* is very different, very different indeed, it is quite numb, quite without feeling, in fact the harder I push the less you feel, just pressure that is all. Very good!' The subject is asked to retain this analgesia in the same way as he retained the hyperaesthesia and the demonstration of the two entirely opposite effects post-hypnotically is most convincing to the subject. The fact that analgesia is more difficult to elicit is undoubtedly rendered easier by starting with hyperaesthesia.

Once hypnotic analgesia has been obtained teaching the subject *auto-analgesia* is a relatively simple matter; the subject is asked to put himself into a trance and it is explained to him that by stroking his left hand from the finger-tips up to the wrist with his right hand whilst he is counting slowly to himself he will be able to make his left hand quite numb, quite insensitive; he is asked to raise the index finger of his left hand when he can feel this numbness to be present. This analgesia may be tested in the usual way by the subject and/or the operator. The subject is requested to retain this analgesia until he comes out of hypnosis so that it may be discussed with him, after which he may abolish it for himself by looking down at the left hand and saying to himself: 'It's gone now.' He awakens himself and is complimented on his achievement and he then abolishes the analgesia.

Finally, he may be told that he can produce this analgesia by merely looking down at his hand, stroking it with the other whilst counting to himself from one to ten and at ten it will be quite numb; he will return it to normal in the same manner as before by looking at the hand and saying to himself: 'It's gone now.' The rationale here being that the subject automatically goes into hypnosis during the production of the analgesia which is afterwards retained as a post-hypnotic suggestion until no longer required.

It will not come amiss at this point to reiterate that any phenomena that have been effected during the course of treatment *must* be removed on termination, for example analgesia in any area must be abolished and arm rigidity must be returned to normal etc.

What is meant by the *Barring-out clause* (the right place and the right time) is explained very carefully in hypnosis and the significance of the patients accomplishment is stressed. The operator has a serious responsibility to the patient to safeguard him from irresponsible people and from himself.

The correct teaching of auto-analgesia is equally as important as it is for auto-hypnosis and for this reason the writer has adopted a standard phraseology: 'Now that you have learned to produce this analgesia, this numbness in any part of your body where it is desirable I want to explain to you how important it is that you do not abuse this privilege in any way.' The observant reader will have noticed that in talking to patients technical or semi-technical terms have often been used: the writer has always thought that, where feasible, it is good practice to educate and explain to the patients. There is no doubt that they are much more co-operative when they are totally involved in the situation, and very little time is needed to achieve this. One continues: 'You will not make any area of your body numb or analgesic except for a doctor or dentist requiring it or for the purpose of demonstration at a scientific meeting or lecture. You will be totally unable to demonstrate the ability you have acquired at a party to amuse your friends and if you develop a pain in any part of your body, be it in a tooth or anywhere else you will take the usual steps to have it attended to as soon as possible, *you will on no account mask this pain*. If you have to have a tooth extracted you may, *with the approval of your dentist only*, give yourself the suggestion that you will experience little if any discomfort in the first 12–18 hours of healing, *but* in the event of appreciable after-pain on the second to third day you will have the cause investigated by the dentist. 'Now I am going to repeat all this to you to make sure that you completely understand it.' After this repetition and before the subject has brought himself out of hypnosis I finally add: '—and now before you open your eyes and wake up, I want you to let me know that you have thoroughly understood all the instructions that have been given you, that you realise they are for your own good, that they are to safeguard your own interests, and that you will faithfully abide by them. I want you to let me know that you agree by just raising the index finger of your left hand.' The ideo-motor signalling obtained in affirmation may be considered of greater significance than verbal confirmation.

The precept has already been stated, although in a slightly different form, that when suggestions are given directly to the subconscious mind and are accepted by the subject as reasonable and for his own good it is extremely unlikely that the conscious mind will be able to override them. A little earlier on in this chapter it was said *à propos* post-operative pain that the patient under certain circumstances could mask this pain:

'*With the approval of your dentist only.*' The reason for this is, of course, that as the patient has been taught auto-hypnosis and auto-analgesia the operator who is treating them at any one time may not be the original teacher. You have quite rightly made them independent of you and they must know *exactly* how to act in all circumstances.

Several points of practical clinical interest arise in the application of hypnotic analgesia. In hypnotic analgesia the subject can at best only interpret an effect as he sees it in his own mind, as he feels he ought to interpret it. You cannot, for example, ask a hypnotised person to manifest all the effects of a mandibular block when he has no idea what you are talking about, but you may expect a good subject who is a dental surgeon *and knows what to expect* to satisfy all your requirements. The writer well remembers his own failure to obtain analgesia in a dental member at a basic course: he had gone into hypnosis during the practical session the afternoon before and had also been taught auto-hypnosis. As he was a dentist, analgesia was suggested by pricking the skin in four places around the wrist with the usual suggestions. Ideo-motor signalling failed to acknowledge any analgesia and on being questioned he said that although he was a dentist he had no *subjective experience of 'locals' in any form* and he felt very worried about interpreting the effect.

Another interesting case of interpretation concerns a female aged 35 who was being treated by the writer's assistant; she was a very intelligent patient and had been trained in auto-hypnosis and analgesia. Her usual procedure was to ask which tooth was to be filled and then to make the area analgesic by transference, grasping the tooth with the finger and thumb and 'kneading' the area somewhat in the manner of amalgamation in a finger-stall; she would then relax herself completely and only come out of the trance when the operator asked her to. On one occasion a distal cavity was being prepared in an upper five and my assistant found a mesial cavity in the six, which he naturally proceeded to prepare. The patient became very restive, brought herself out of the trance and said: 'I can feel that!' and then, after a short pause, while she explored with her tongue: 'You're doing the next tooth, you never told me and I have not made it numb!' She proceeded to make the six analgesic, went back into a trance and everything went smoothly. It is important to remember that any instructions given to the patient in hypnosis *must* be unequivocal, they should *never* be capable of misinterpretation.

Some years ago I was lacking a volunteer to demonstrate analgesia at a basic course and our then National Secretary of the B.S.M.D.H. came on to the platform. A circle about the size of a penny was drawn on the back of his hand with a biro and a very effective analgesia was produced by pricking the circumference of the circle in four places with the suggestion that it would soon become numb like a good local anaesthetic; this was indeed so but when I tried to demonstrate that the area immediately outside the circle was *not* analgesic I ran into difficulties as the numbness extended over a very large area outside the circle: on being questioned he said: 'You know and I know that if you ring round a circle with a local anaesthetic it spreads all over the place!'—a lay person will make the area inside the circumference quite numb if asked to do so but immediately *outside* the circumferential line the skin will be sensitive. This illustrates very well how a person in hypnosis interprets the various phenomena subjectively according to his own field of experience.

John Hartland in *Medical and Dental Hypnosis* recounts a very interesting case concerning analgesia. A young married woman was taught auto-hypnosis for her confinement; she would readily go into a deep trance but to his surprise it was found impossible to effect any degree of analgesia. She became involved in a motor accident and suffered acute pain in her right arm and shoulder. Her husband left her sitting by the roadside whilst he hurried to get assistance; on his return, to his amazement, he found she had put herself into a hypnotic trance and abolished all pain and discomfort. Hartland has this to say: 'It must, therefore, sometimes be possible for hypnosis to secure complete relief from pain arising from pathological or physiological processes in cases in which it was impossible to produce any marked degree of insensitivity to pain caused by an artificial external stimulus.'

In this connection the writer would like to quote the case of his own receptionist—she had been taught auto-hypnosis and could attain a moderate depth of trance but all attempts to produce any degree of analgesia failed. She had occasion to have a lower eight extracted and when my associate was about to give her a mandibular injection she said that she did not require it, he could just take it out. He very reluctantly proceeded to do so and the tooth was removed with a Winter's elevator with little difficulty. During the operation my receptionist sat quite still in the chair with closed eyes; on being questioned she said that the extraction had caused her no pain, she did not *expect* it to cause her any pain, she just accepted the fact that the tooth had to be extracted and she furthermore volunteered the information that *if she had to have the eight out on the other side she would unhesitatingly choose the same method!*

The importance of the correct teaching of both auto-hypnosis and auto-analgesia has been stressed in this chapter and it has been made clear, in the writer's opinion, that of these two phenomena auto-hypnosis is obligatory. Auto-analgesia cannot be taught to all subjects but auto-hypnosis can and it alone will facilitate dental treatment to a very marked degree, a degree that almost always permits treatment to be carried out in a routine manner, locals being used if necessary, although the attendant pain threshold is generally so raised that local anaesthesia is much more rarely resorted to. It is timely to point out that some patients who have been taught auto-hypnosis find that after some time they no longer need hypnosis in treatment; they have become so conditioned, as it were, that they are able to accept all forms of dental treatment with equanimity. This is a very rewarding aspect of hypnotic training, especially rewarding for the operator.

CHAPTER 7

Some Case Histories

THESE case histories have been chosen to present as wide a range as possible, and have all been taken from patients in an average busy practice: what noticably emerges from a study of these histories over the years is the marked individual variation in reaction to any given stimulus. The impossiblity of classifying or pigeon-holing all the reactions of subjects in the hypnotic situation is nowhere more clearly seen than in the dental chair—a formula may be learned and once learned applied in every case, but only experience will enable the practitioner to approach the varying types of individuals he encounters in everyday practice with growing confidence.

Before itemising actual cases it is timely to mention here the importance of carefully taking the patient's medical and previous dental history. This does not take very long and may be of inestimable value at a later date.

It has been pointed out that the dangers of hypnosis in dental practice have been grossly exaggerated; this is true *but* a few judicious enquiries into past medical history (any serious illnesses etc.) and if any dental experience in particular is remembered disadvantageously may serve as a safeguarding guide during the course of treatment. Mention may be made here of what is known as *Feedback*: on questioning the subject after his initial induction he may say it was a wonderful experience—'As though I were floating along completely carefree on a fleecy white cloud' or he may say something quite different but equally suggestive of a complete and pleasant state of relaxation. Whatever it is you may, with advantage, 'feed it back' to him on his next visit: it has been the writer's experience for a patient to say on the second visit: 'I hope I shall have the same lovely feeling this time as I had on my last visit.'

Case 1

LINDA—a lively intelligent child, aged 8. She accepted treatment but very reluctantly. 'I think your drill is horrible!' She was asked if she would like to close her eyes and dream about her favourite TV programme and not worry about having her teeth done: she expressed willingness and chose 'Rawhide', a current TV Western. Arm levitation was quickly achieved and further deepening was carried out by means of arm heaviness and arm rigidity. A post-hypnotic was given her to the effect that she would go back into hypnosis by looking at the operator's pen which was held up in front of her as he counted from 1 to 5. Awakened by counting backwards from 5 to 1. She went back into hypnosis on the prearranged signal. *No treatment was carried out on this visit.*

The second visit was a week later and Linda was quickly taught analgesia of the left hand by the glove-analogy method. This analgesia was transferred to the D\ in the usual way and a local given to extract the tooth. The subject exhibited no reaction of any kind and on awakening had no recollection of the event.

On the third visit Linda asked to look at 'Robin Hood' instead of 'Rawhide'. Analgesia was transferred from the hand to the area around /E and on testing was found to be complete and the tooth was extracted under hypnotic analgesia; the only noticeable reaction was a slight blushing on the cheeks: on awakening she was surprised to find that the tooth had been extracted.

This child was treated for some two years when her parents left the district. She never presented any problems and it was interesting to note that she chose to vary her visualisation from time to time according to her whim.

Case 2

JOY—a married woman, aged 36. She had a very low threshold of pain and would react to the slightest degree of instrumentation, gagging being a prominent feature. She was given a short talk explaining the advantages of relaxation in raising the pain threshold (she was a part-time nurse) and, as she had to have a partial upper denture, impressions were taken with some difficulty and she agreed to try hypnosis.

The coin technique was successfully employed and she was unable to raise her arm on suggestions of arm heaviness. Her appointment time had been considerably overrun and she was told she would wake up very pleased with her experience on the third deep breath. No post-hypnotic for future induction was given. On awakening she expressed herself very pleased with her experience.

A week later she was induced by arm levitation and analgesia of the right hand was produced; she was given a post-hypnotic for future induction looking at her hands while the operator counted from 1 to 5. Brought out of trance by counting from 5 to 1. Was very pleased with her success, especially the analgesia which had been retained as a post-hypnotic for demonstration. Put back into trance and further assurances given for complete success, lack of fear and improvement with each visit.

It was decided to fit her P/ on her third visit and it was explained to her that as she could transfer analgesia from her hand to the tooth area she need have no worry at all about the actual act of injection; she doubted this but was told there was no room for doubt and that failure was impossible. Hypnosis was induced and analgesia of hand transferred to the /23 area with repeated assurances that when she woke up she could retain this numbness and have her injection without any worry at all and the same would apply to her extractions. Immediately on awakening the labial injection was given, the patient closed her eyes and gave no sign that she was aware of anything being done. After a moment or so she opened her eyes and said: 'When are you going to give me the injection?' The teeth were extracted and the P/ fitted to the patient's great satisfaction. She was put back into hypnosis and told that she would soon get used to the denture, that healing would be uneventful and that the analgesia would soon disappear. From this time on her treatment pursued a routine pattern *but* on her sixth visit some two months after her first hypnotic induction she said: 'I do not need hypnosis any more for my dental treatment; you have taught me to relax and I now feel I can accept anything that is necessary in my mouth.'

This case is a very interesting one in reference to the writer's remarks at the end of the chapter on auto-hypnosis and analgesia.

Case 3

DAVID—this boy was 12 years old, a nail-biter and very anxious to overcome the habit: he was above the average in intelligence. Induced by eye-fixation, eyes soon closing. Deepening by inability to raise arm followed by arm levitation. It was then again and again stressed that as he was now 12 years old this habit of nail-biting no longer served any purpose and he would abandon the habit. He was further told that when he was watching the TV and his hand went up to his mouth, he would remember what had been told him and he would *not* bite his nails but just rub his chin once or twice and then lower his hand: 'You will do this three or four times in the course of watching the TV and soon you will come to realise that it is pointless to keep rubbing your chin and you will find that you don't need to bite your nails or rub your chin and you will be very, very pleased about it indeed, so pleased that the next time you come you will tell me you have conquered this habit directly you come into the surgery.' On his next visit, a fortnight later, he eagerly told the writer that he had succeeded and was very pleased about it.

In cases of nail-biting and thumb-sucking where the condition has lingered on to become a habit long after it has ceased to serve a useful purpose, if indeed it ever had one, then direct suggestion under hypnosis may have spectacular results.

At David's second visit further deepening was carried out and reinforcing suggestions were given.

Case 4

JENNIFER—married, aged 21. No treatment for some years; she explained this as due to extreme fear of dental treatment but could offer no logical reason. She had been referred by her general practitioner as she was pregnant.

She was a very pleasant, seemingly intelligent girl, but it was noted that she was somewhat obese. Her dental condition showed one of extreme neglect and most of her upper teeth were not capable of conservation. Hypnosis was explained to her and she said she was keen to try it as she realised something would have to be done about her mouth.

Trance soon induced by eye-fixation, deepened by breathing exercises and heaviness of arm. Awakened after post-hypnotic for future induction looking at operator's pen while counting 1 to 5. On coming out of trance patient said she was very pleased with the experience. Re-induced and arm levitation followed by arm rigidity successfully performed. Analgesia of the right hand by glove analogy; this was very marked and was retained for demonstration to the patient. She was very delighted with the analgesic effect and had no hesitation in testing it for herself with a dental probe.

On her second visit 10 days later further deepening was carried out and analgesia in the hand was transferred to the 32/ area including the lip. The patient was very impressed with the marked numbness of the area and readily accepted the suggestion that this could be the preliminary to a local anaesthetic. As an immediate denture was to be made, the analgesia was abolished around 32/ and transferred to 765/ and these teeth were extracted with no reaction on the part of the patient. Further extractions took place on subsequent visits and the immediate denture fitted.

When the patient came for her final visit to have her fillings, she said that she did not think she could go through with it as in her mind she had regarded fillings as being worse than extractions and 'I don't want to break down now'.

After a careful explanation aimed at restoring her confidence she was put into a trance—the assurance being given that no fillings would be attempted until she was willing, quite willing to have them done. Now follows a verbatim account of the procedure adopted in this case:

'I want you to imagine that you are looking through a wide-open door and as you do so into the room beyond you notice that it is a dentist's surgery, the room is brightly lit and you see the dentist leaning over the chair in which a patient is seated; the patient is a young girl of about twenty. Now I want you to look closely and nod your head to tell me you see this picture clearly. Good! very good! the dentist is doing a filling, you know this because you can hear the faint high-pitched whine of the high-speed drill [at this stage the drill is turned on for a few moments] which he has in his hand. You have the feeling that you are watching the scene in a detached sort of way as though you were a spectator watching a film in the cinema. You become curious to see more and you come forward into the room so that you can see the patient better. This young girl's eyes are closed and, although her mouth is open, there is a look of complete repose on her countenance; it is as though she were absolutely at peace, calm and contented and you look down at her hands which are lying in her lap, the fingers slightly bent. There is a complete absence of tension about this patient and you come right up to the chair, turn round and look right into the patient's face and suddenly you realise you can identify her, you know who this girl is who is sitting there, so calm, so relaxed and absolutely unworried. You feel very pleased indeed and a smile breaks over your face even as you look at her' [a smile breaks over the subject's face].

'I want you to tell me who it is that you are looking at, sitting there so relaxed and calm in the dental chair. Tell me who she is please.' There is a long pause and then very quietly, almost inaudibly and very slowly, Jennifer says: 'It's me!'

'Yes, it's you sitting there so calm and relaxed and now you know that all your fears are conquered and you have nothing, absolutely nothing to be afraid of any more; you are very, very pleased indeed. I want you to nod your head to let me know that you have overcome all your fears.' There is again a long pause and Jennifer slowly nods her head.

When she came out of the trance she expressed her willingness to have her fillings done and the rest of her treatment was uneventful.

There is an interesting sequel to this case—some months later, after she had had her baby, she came along for a dental inspection and volunteered the information that her delivery had been completely free of complications as she had been able to carry out all the suggestions given her in the same manner that she had been able to carry them out for me. When the nursing staff complimented her on being such an excellent patient she told them it was all due to her dentist teaching her to relax! Critics could say in this instance that the writer had not confined his hypnotic treatment to his own particular discipline!

This case does, of course, involve dissociation and there is an element of danger that, in a schizophrenic, a complete breakdown may be caused, but in the case of a subject who has behaved in a hitherto normal manner and of whom the dentist has a good history from either the patient's general practitioner or *his own notes* there should be little cause for anxiety.

Case 5

MARGARET was $13\frac{1}{2}$ years old when she first came to the practice; she was an only child and her parents had been patients for some two years and had both stated that it was impossible to get her to come to the dentist, the mother saying: 'I don't know why, I can't think why, my husband and I have never minded coming'—the last part of that statement was certainly true but that was the only part.

Margaret was a shy, somewhat withdrawn child, but on promising faithfully not to do any treatment, it was possible, if only cursorily, with the aid of a mirror to inspect her mouth, but well-nigh impossible to retract the upper or lower lip to examine the labial surfaces of the incisors.

Despite her extreme tension and fear she would answer questions quietly but readily and intelligently: when asked if she could remember any reason or definite incident that may have caused her fear Margaret said that she could not think of anything at all. The benefits of relaxation were then explained to her and on promising once again to refrain from any treatment until she was quite ready she agreed to hypnosis and proved to be a good subject.

Minor deepening exercises were carried out and the usual post-hypnotic for re-induction given. On the next visit, a week later, she at once entered a trance, further deepening resulting in a good analgesia of the hand. She was then asked to open her mouth but immediately became very agitated; she was calmed, told not to worry and that she need not open her mouth if she did not wish to do so. Questioning under hypnosis as to the reason for her reluctance to open her mouth produced the simple statement: 'I don't know.'

Margaret was then told that before she came the next time she would have a dream and that this dream would reveal to her the cause of her fear. The dream would not frighten her in any way; she would see it as though she were a member of the audience in a cinema or theatre. She was further told that she might even forget it for a while but that she would remember it the moment she came into the surgery on the next visit: it could then be talked over and shown to her that all her fears were now quite groundless.

On her next visit Margaret volunteered the information that she did dream and now knew why she was afraid of the dentist. Some years earlier she had had toothache and was taken to the dentist who asked her to open her mouth and in her own words —'He just pulled my tooth out without anything, *he did not even tell me he was going to do it*!' and a later memory was 'that I was almost dragged to the dentist who tried to fill a tooth without telling me what he was doing!' She would not let him and soon afterwards she had an anaesthetic and four sixes were removed. From this time on her parents were unable to get her to go to the dentist.

In the waking state it was explained to Margaret that this was all in the past and that now she had no cause for alarm as nothing would ever be done to her without an explanation and with her approval, furthermore now that she had learned to relax so well treatment would no longer worry her.

Further explanations were given in hypnosis and she consented to have dental treatment; this was carried out with very little difficulty. She was taught auto-hypnosis and seven years later was transferred to one of the associates in the practice and her dental sessions proceeded normally.

It is of considerable interest to note that twice Margaret complained that she had received nothing in the way of an explanation from the practitioner. The moral in this is obvious.

Case 6

JACQUELINE, aged 19, had been referred by a colleague owing to a needle phobia: her dental condition had been poor and the practitioner who was treating her found it difficult to carry out all her treatment as he was unable to use locals for the sensitive teeth. She was a quiet, shy girl, very anxious to co-operate and overcome her fear. Past history revealed that she had never had a dental injection and that, as far back as she could remember, had always fainted or had had 'an hysterical attack' whenever she had had an injection for any purpose. No reason for her aversion could be given, and as she was impatient to have her mouth put in order as soon as possible, it was decided to by-pass the needle phobia for the present and to concentrate on raising the pain threshold as much as feasible by hypnotic training.

Induction soon achieved by the dropped-coin technique and after simple deepening exercises glove analgesia was produced and retained as a post-hypnotic for demonstration. Jacqueline was very impressed with this manifestation and so she was taught auto-hypnosis on this first visit.

On the second visit she was asked *in hypnosis* if she knew of any reason why she was so frightened by an injection but could give none, but furthering questioning revealed that she felt her fear to be deep-seated as 'she could accept a fair amount of pain but this was different'.

Auto-analgesia was now explained to her and also the significance of transference from one area to another. She was quickly able to do this for herself, transferring numbness of the hand to the 2| area (this was chosen as being a very 'impressive' area to demonstrate). Jacqueline described this as feeling like cotton wool. Her conduct on seeking treatment with her dentist was thoroughly explained to her—this was done both in and out of hypnosis and as she had proved so apt a subject it was suggested that she was now ready to fix an appointment for her conservative treatment: to this she willingly agreed and promised to contact the practice later to report her progress.

As nothing was heard from this patient after many weeks, her dentist was contacted who reported that he had seen her and carried out considerable conservative work while she was in hypnosis and 'would never have believed it possible'. This case may be regarded as successful insofar that, owing to the patient being a good hypnotic subject, the necessity for local anaesthesia was avoided: the needle phobia had, of course, not been dealt with and it was ascertained a little later in a telephonic communication with the mother that Jacqueline did not wish to pursue the matter any further.

Case 7.

JACKIE was a particularly lively and intelligent child of 12 when first seen; she had a very low threshold of pain and was eager to be taught to relax.

She was induced by eye-fixation and very quickly became a

deep trance subject, dental treatment being merely a matter of routine.

One day in the course of her treatment Jackie said that she had a confession to make: it was to the effect that she had gone to a party and told her friends that all her dental work was done when she was in hypnosis and, furthermore, her dentist had taught her auto-hypnosis so that she was able to put herself into a trance. Somewhat flattered at the interest shown by the young audience she sat down in a chair, looked down at her hands lying in her lap and commenced to count aloud from 1 to 5; nothing happened, she tried again with still no result and at the third attempt she gave it up, her party spirit being somewhat deflated. This event took place some two years after her first treatment under hypnosis and is included in these case histories purely to show the importance and success of the barring-out clause in safeguarding the patient's interests.

It may be pointed out that Jackie's case is unusual in that, although it is obligatory to safeguard the patient's interests, it is very seldom put to the test. Initially subjects may often be fascinated by their ability to go into hypnosis, but they very soon come to accept this capability as a normal part of dental treatment.

Case 8

KATHLEEN was a bright intelligent woman of 30, married with no children: she had been attending a clinic for migraine, having been a sufferer for some years. She volunteered the information that she was very frightened of dental treatment.

Relaxed by eye-fixation which was quickly achieved: then asked to visualise a balloon tied to her right hand by a piece of white string and—'the string is quite taut and you can feel it pulling on your hand. Tell me, what is the colour of your balloon? Red! I see. Now as you watch the balloon closely you realise that your arm is beginning to float up into the air, pulled up by the balloon, lighter and lighter', etc. The opposite effect of arm heaviness was then produced with consequent inability to raise the arm. Post-hypnotic suggestion for re-induction given and awakened. Expressed herself very pleased with her relaxation.

On the second visit deepening exercises were carried out using Wolberg's variations in cutaneous sensibility. Hyperaesthesia was very marked and analgesia was profound, the subject herself volunteering the information: 'I'm sure it's numb all through!' In hypnosis she was given a talk on her ability to have all her treatment under hypnosis and be very pleased about it.

On her third visit Kathleen was taught auto-hypnosis with the usual safeguards and it was explained to her how she could have use of it at home when she felt she needed to relax.

Her fourth visit was for the extraction of 21/12 with the insertion of an immediate P/. These teeth were very unsightly, had been heavily filled and there was marked superior protrusion; the patient had long expressed a wish to be rid of them.

In spite of this wish she said she was dreading this visit as she had always been frightened of extractions.

After a preliminary discussion aimed at reassuring her she put herself into hypnosis and hypnotic analgesia of the 21/12 area was produced by rubbing the area with the thumb and forefinger palatally and labially. A local injection was then given with absolutely no reaction from the patient. The P/ was fitted, a small pack inserted in the labial sulcus and left for a few minutes to arrest ensuing haemorrhage. On being awakened and shown her mouth in a mirror, she expressed herself delighted and added that she did not know when her teeth had been extracted.

All her future treatment pursued a normal course and when she was transferred to one of my associates she was regarded as a model patient.

Case 9

Mrs. D—. This last case history has been chosen to show specially how and why a particularly good, albeit somewhat lengthy, method of induction fails in a subject who may well prove capable of manifesting a medium trance with a different approach.

Mrs. D. was aged 42 and had suffered from bouts of depression from time to time. The impression gained on the preliminary interview was one of below normal intelligence: she had been referred by her general practitioner in order to have a full upper denture made, all her upper teeth having been extracted some months previously under a general anaesthetic. She refused, however, all attempts to take an impression owing to an irrational fear of suffocation—this fear completely overriding her earnest desire to wear a denture.

It was decided, erroneously as it later proved, to induce hypnosis by means of Erickson's arm levitation. After some 15 minutes during which time she stared fixedly at her stiff and motionless fingers she suddenly turned to the writer and said: 'It's no good, I've always been ashamed of my hands!' On critically regarding her hands, something the writer had not previously thought about, it was noticed that they were indeed very work-stained and unattractive. After suitable apologies, eye-fixation with distraction was chosen as an alternative and the subject quickly went into hypnosis and normal deepening exercises were successful.

Suggestions aimed at encouraging her to face her treatment with equanimity were then given, one explanation being that things which previously had worried her appreciably, *like the taking of an impression or the mere thought of doing so*, would no longer worry her because this was the great benefit of learning to relax. It was further explained that the next time she came she would be able to relax immediately and even more deeply when asked to do so, and furthermore she would be very pleased about it, very pleased indeed. A post-hypnotic for future induction was given and the patient awakened: she expressed herself very pleased at learning to relax—'Something I never thought I'd be able to do!'

Before dismissal she was, *as all subjects are*, put back into hypnosis for a short period by the post-hypnotic signal previously arranged.

On her second visit the *modus operandi* of impression taking was carefully explained to the subject. The trays were shown and a small amount of material was mixed and inserted into a tray to demonstrate the relative stiffness and control obtained under all circumstances. She was told that she would be able to breathe IN—and—OUT slowly all the time her impression was being taken and that I would time her breathing for her by saying IN—OUT and that she must pay particular attention to my timing as it was most important in abolishing the gag reflex.

Finally, it was explained to her that she had learned to relax very well and therefore *failure was impossible.*

All this was repeated to the patient in the hypnotic state: the treatment was then proceeded with and no difficulty of any kind was encountered.

In timing her breathing by saying aloud IN—OUT from time to time the words VERY—GOOD were substituted occasionally thus: IN—OUT; IN—OUT; VERY—GOOD; IN—OUT; VERY—GOOD.

On coming out of hypnosis and fully realising her success the patient broke down and cried for a short time—in this case a very healthy sign!

The discerning reader on studying this last case may well say the writer was lucky in his success, that the patient may have come out of hypnosis at the critical moment and refused all further treatment. This is indeed true and another approach would have been to attempt to recall in hypnosis any traumatic incident relating to taking an impression and if not directly successful to have turned to dream recall as in Case 5.

This was not done because the writer felt the excellent degree of relaxation secured and the ready acceptance by the subject of the practical demonstration and explanation of the taking of impressions would result in a successful issue: this proved here to be the case.

CHAPTER 8

Conclusion

In this short work the writer hopes that he has shown hypnosis to be more than worth while in dental practice—no claim is made that it is a panacea, psychological or otherwise, for all the difficulties encountered in practice, but the claim *is* made that hypnosis, and here the writer would include *the approach to the patient*, ought to form part of the normal training of the student to be used as and when necessary.

Postgraduate courses are undoubtedly of great value and the *British Society of Medical and Dental Hypnosis* has done splendid work in furthering the cause of hypnosis in medicine and dentistry and the holding of talks at the monthly meetings of BDA and BMA Sections should not be forgotten, but until hypnosis is included in the student's curriculum it will not take its rightful place in medicine and dentistry along with radiology, anaesthesia etc.

'The hypnotic approach' is subconsciously used by most perceptive dental surgeons: it requires very little training for them to implement fully the psychological understanding they already possess resulting in an almost, if not quite, total acceptance of all forms of treatment to the great benefit of the patient and to the satisfaction of the operator.

Owing to a complete lack of training in matters psychological, the average dental student embarks on his career having acquired a high degree of technical skill, but with an abysmal ignorance pertaining to matters of the mind; it is only by a laborious process of empiricism that he may slowly acquire the necessary knowledge.

Now this is unnecessary and the inclusion of lectures on psychology, psychosomatics and hypnosis in the student's curriculum is not a practical impossibility: it is said that the curriculum is already overburdened and that technological advances in both disciplines have not left any room for further periods of study.

It is indeed true to say that dentistry in particular has seen sweeping advances in practical treatment in the last 25 years, but the study of psychosomatics has scarcely touched the profession in this country, and an appreciable number of patients, and especially children, will not always submit readily to our ministrations.

The writer considers that if twelve periods of $\frac{1}{2}$–$\frac{3}{4}$ hour were devoted to lectures on psychosomatics and hypnosis the student would have at least a reasonable working knowledge of the subject, and by working knowledge is meant the possession of sufficient knowledge to approach the nervous and apprehensive patient with real feeling; then, and only then, would be begin to understand the real meaning of *empathy* and *rapport*.

Interpersonal relationship plays a very strong part in the practice of medicine and dentistry, so strong a part that it is no exaggeration to say that, carefully "manipulated" in the best sense of the word, it is capable of raising the pain threshold appreciably. The patient who has come to believe in you, who has complete faith in you, expects that it will come about as you predict, when you explain that what you are about to do will be easily tolerated: one recalls to mind a not-uncommon remark made by such patients: 'Well if you say so, Mr. X., I'm sure it will be all right.'

The right approach to the patient may well be inherent in some fortunate operators, *but it may be taught in others to great advantage*. There is indeed no difficulty in teaching the average student how best to approach the patient.

Why then is this not done? It is difficult really to believe that, however crowded the curriculum, a few hours cannot be found for this important subject and this has always been the reason put forward when the matter has been broached.

Thus the increasing acceptance of hypnosis in medicine and dentistry is being slowly brought about by a small group of enthusiastic lecturers at BMA and BDA meetings, the courses held throughout the country by the British Society of Medical and Dental Hypnosis and a handful of lectures arranged by the Postgraduate Medical and Dental Federation.

To substantiate the earlier claim made in this chapter that hypnosis is worth while the following is offered:

The writer was in Australia in 1973 and lectured in Brisbane at the dental school on hypnosis. Dr. Charles Elliott, a member of the BSMDH, who kindly acted as host, showed the writer a letter he had received from a young patient of his; he had trained her using picture visualisation to go to the dentist and visualise her own TV programme. This letter which is from a photostat of the original speaks for itself (*see* Frontispiece).

INDEX